VERITAS ET UTILITAS

# Learning to Lead

in celebration
of seven decades of
business education
at Western, 1923-93

# Learning

Generously funded,
in full, by
Xerox Canada Inc.

# to Lead

Western Business School
The University of Western Ontario
1923-1993

A tribute to those, past and present, who have encouraged the quest for leadership in business.

A collection of memories by some of those who have helped lay the foundation of Western Business School.

*The Ivey family of London have, for three generations, played a generous, leadership role in the development of Western Business School. Richard G. Ivey, who helped establish this first, national school of business was Chancellor of The University of Western Ontario (1955-1961). His daughter, Mrs. Lorraine Shuttleworth, through the Richard and Jean Ivey Fund, has long been a benefactor. His son, Richard M. Ivey, pictured here, in addition to his personal involvement and support of the School, was Chancellor (1980-1984). His son, Richard W. Ivey and daughter, Mrs. Rosamond Thom, both graduates of the School, continue the Ivey tradition by taking an active interest in the School as it prepares for the 21st century.*

Western's mace has been used throughout this book to denote a citation, read by Western's president, about the person being conferred with a degree from the University.

Western's mace was presented to the University at the installation of Dr. G. Edward Hall as President and Vice-Chancellor in 1948 to mark the seventieth anniversary of the University. Originally, maces were used as war clubs and later evolved as symbols of corporate identity and authority. It is used at convocation ceremonies and is placed before the chancellor.

## Collected & Edited by Doreen Sanders C.M.

DESIGN
LESLIE SMART & ASSOCIATES LIMITED

PRINTED IN CANADA

# Contents

# Highlights of the development of Western Business School

**1922** Teaching of business administration begun at Western (known as Commercial Economics)

Ellis H. Morrow appointed Head of Department of Commercial Economics, Faculty of Arts (located on former Huron College campus)

**1923** First B.A. (Honors Commerce) granted

**1924** The University of Western Ontario moved from Huron College campus to its present site on the bank of the Thames River

**1927** Dr. W. Sherwood Fox installed as President and Vice-Chancellor of the University

Department of Commercial Economics name changed to Department of Business Administration, Faculty of Arts

**1929** Philip H. Hensel appointed Head of Department

**1932** Graduate work in Business begun

**1933** *Quarterly Review of Commerce* begun publishing. Later, title changed to *The Business Quarterly*

**1938** Walter A. Thompson appointed Acting Head of the Department

First Alumni Directory published listing 196 names of business graduates

**1942** Ross B. Willis appointed Acting Head of the Department

**1947** Dr. G. Edward Hall installed as President and Vice-Chancellor of the University

**1948** In March, 100 Canadian businessmen met at Western to discuss the need for a national school of business administration

Management Training Course established, Walter A. Thompson, founding Director. This marked the first of the Continuing Education Courses offered to business

**1950** School of Business Administration established (located in lower hall of University College)

Lloyd W. Sipherd appointed first Dean

Board of Governors established School's Advisory Committee

R.G. Ivey, Q.C. appointed first Chairman of Committee

First Master of Business Administration degree granted

**1951** School moved to Goodholme, a former residence, off campus

**1953** First Marketing Management Course offered to businessmen, J.J. Wettlaufer, founding Director

**1954** F.W.P. Jones appointed Dean

**1955** J.R. White appointed Chairman of Advisory Committee

**1957** Official opening of Richard Ivey School of Business Administration Building on campus

First annual 'London Conference' inaugurated

**1960** Larger library facilities added to the building

**1961** Senate approved first Ph.D Program in business in Canada

W. Harold Rae appointed Chairman of Advisory Committee

**1963** J.J. Wettlaufer appointed Dean

**1964** First Ph.D. degree in business conferred on Alexander Mikalachki

Ford Foundation awards five-year grant in support of the Ph.D Program

**1967** Dr. D. Carlton Williams installed as President and Vice-Chancellor of the University

Second Alumni Directory listing 5,927 alumni of the School published to mark Canada's Centennial

Computer and the Manager Course offered, Andrew A. Grindlay, founding Director

**1968** John E. Brent appointed Chairman of Advisory Committee

**1969** New addition to the School is completed doubling size of the building

Richard Ivey Foundation and Richard and Jean Ivey Fund provided grant for computer equipment and MBA and Ph.D Fellowships

**1970** 'Plan for Excellence' started to raise $1.5 million for research and MBA and Ph.D Fellowship Programs

Production and Operations Management Course offered, A.R. (Bert) Wood, founding Director

**1971** Five-year agreement signed with the Canadian International Development Agency and the University of the West Indies to assist in development of management studies programs on Jamaica and Trinidad campuses

**1972** Small Business Assistance Program begun supported by Ontario Ministry of Industry and Tourism, John Graham, John Kennedy and George Forsyth, founding Directors

**1973** Birthday Parties held with alumni across Canada and abroad to celebrate School's fiftieth anniversary

Indian Business Assistance Program established across Canada sponsored by Department of Indian Affairs and Northern Development, John Graham, founding Director

**1974** Western Arctic Program offered for first time sponsored by Imperial Oil and Arctic Gas for the pilot project

Centre for International Business Studies established under five-year grant from Department of Industry, Trade and Commerce, Harold Crookell, Director

**1975** The first Brazilian Management Course offered in that country, John Nicholson, founding Director

'Plan for Excellence', Phase II, established to raise $2.1 million for research and MBA and Ph.D Fellowships

Managerial Accounting and Control for Financial Executives Program offered, T.R. (Ross) Archibald, founding Director

First Western Business School Club organized in Toronto

**1976** Senior University Administrators' Course established and supported by grants from Kellogg Foundation and Richard and Jean Ivey Fund, J.J. DiStefano, founding Director

Col. Allan Burton appointed Chairman of Advisory Committee

**1977** Dr. George E. Connell installed as President and Vice-Chancellor of the University

**1978** The University of Western Ontario celebrated its one hundredth anniversary

C.B. Johnston appointed Dean

Spencer Hall Continuing Education Centre officially opened

International Management Course established at Western, Harold Crookell, founding Director

Grant received from the Richard Ivey Foundation to establish the Richard G. Ivey Computing Centre

**1979** New Ivey Computer Centre opened 'Plan for Excellence', Phase III, announced to begin in 1980 to raise $3 million over 1980-1984 period

**1980** John A. (Jack) Armstrong appointed Chairman of Advisory Committee

**1982** Richard G. Ivey Computer Centre upgraded by grant from the Richard Ivey Foundation

**1983** Sixtieth anniversary of the founding of the teaching of business administration at The University of Western Ontario

*Business Quarterly* celebrated its fiftieth year of continuous publication

First Canada/Kenya Executive Management Program offered in that country, Harry Lane, founding Director

James C. Taylor Distinguished Lecture in Finance established

Senior Executive Program offered, J.N. (Nick) Fry, founding Director

Ralph M. Barford appointed Chairman of Advisory Committee

Management of Human Resources Course offered, Jeffrey Gandz, founding Director

**1984** A.K. Adlington installed as Acting President and Vice-Chancellor of the University for 1984-1985

The National Centre for Management Research and Development (NCMRD) established by a $4 million grant from the federal government. Also supported by a $1.5 million commitment from the 'Plan for Excellence' and $3 million from The University of Western Ontario and $3.5 million to be raised from the private sector

Four-year China Program agreement with Tsinghua University signed. Funded by Canadian International Development Agency (CIDA), J.J. DiStefano, founding Director

Hewlett-Packard (Canada) Ltd. made a significant donation of personal computers

**1985**
Dr. George Pedersen installed as President and Vice-Chancellor of the University

Dr. David S.R. Leighton appointed first Director of the NCMRD

First Professorship at NCMRD established by Magna International Inc.

IBM Canada Ltd. donated a mainframe, terminals, PCs, software and peripheral hardware for student use and faculty research

Professorship in Marketing established by Nabisco Brands Ltd.

William G. Davis Chair in International Trade established – to alternate between Business School and Department of Economics

**1986**
NCMRD building completed

R.A. Barford Professorship in Marketing Communications established at NCMRD

The Imperial Life Professorship in Organization Behavior established at NCMRD

Donald G. Campbell appointed Chairman of the Advisory Committee

**1987**
F.W.P. Jones Corridor, a gift of the D.D.C. McGeachy Family and McGeachy Foundation, opened

The Royal Bank Professorship in International Business established at NCMRD

**1988**
Donald F. Hunter Professorship in International Business established by Maclean Hunter Ltd.

Executive Marketing Program for technology-based businesses offered, Adrian B. Ryans, founding Director

Hewlett-Packard (Canada) Ltd. upgraded personal computers and donated printers and software

**1989**
Second five-year contract signed for CIDA-sponsored China Program

The Hewlett-Packard Professorship in Technology Management established

The J. Allyn Taylor and Arthur H. Mingay Chair in Business Administration endowed by The Canada Trust Company

Alexander Mikalachki appointed Acting Dean

**1990**
Adrian B. Ryans appointed Dean

Richard J. Currie elected Chairman of the Advisory Committee

HBA International Case Tournament established

**1991**
Executive Development Centre, established by Western Business School, opened in Mississauga, Ontario. Named the J.J. Wettlaufer Executive Development Centre

Executive MBA Program offered, J.P. (Peter) Killing, founding Director

**1992**
South Wing of Spencer Hall completed for use by all residential executive programs

J.J. Wettlaufer Faculty Fellowship established

F.W.P. Jones Faculty Fellowship established

**1993**
Earl H. Orser appointed Chairman of the Advisory Committee

J.J. Wettlaufer Executive Development Centre in Mississauga purchased with Renaissance Campaign donations, including a major gift from the Richard Ivey Foundation and Ivey Family members

The *Journal of International Business Studies* begins its five-year term at the Western Business School

Purchasing Management Association of Canada Chair in Purchasing Management established at the Western Business School

# Ten-foot square beginnings

*Together, in 1919, two Classics scholars at The University of Western Ontario, Dr. W. Sherwood Fox, then Dean of Arts and Science and Dr. K.P.R. Neville, at the time Registrar, played key roles in establishing what is today, Western Business School.*

*In 1958, Dr. Fox, then in his eightieth year, recalled, in his elegant handwriting on a fifteen-cent note-pad, his memory of events that laid the foundation of teaching business, by the Harvard 'case system', at Western.*

The establishment of the particular type of course which has now become the School of Business Administration of The University of Western Ontario was the result of careful observation and study. When I became Dean of Arts and Science in 1919 the Registrar, Dr. K.P.R. Neville, and I undertook jointly to scrutinize systematically the substance of the applications for admission into the faculty over which I presided. Naturally, a large majority of the applicants were men who had just been discharged from the several war services. Many of them clearly stated that their ultimate goal was a business career and preferred to enter it via an academic route which, though involving more time than a direct approach, would afford an opportunity for formal education which the war had compelled them to forego. One thing in particular impressed us both: a general expression of desire for a course in business, leading not to the degree of Bachelor of Commerce already not uncommon in Canada, but to the degree of Bachelor of Arts with Business option. This preference reflected clearly the common desire for more formal education of the traditional university type.

It soon became all too obvious that Western had nothing to offer applicants with such specific aims – at least for the present. Since our Senate had not yet even considered such an offering, our negative answer turned many young people of Western Ontario to older universities offering the Bachelor of Commerce degree. This diversion gave us food for thought. Perhaps, however, some offering could be found in the near future. So a comprehensive study of all recognized business courses of university grade in North America was at once undertaken and the findings spread on a large sheet 10 feet square. This made a comparative analysis of all offerings both easy and clear.

In due time deliberation yielded crucial conclusions. Outstanding was our judgment that the course given at the Harvard School of Business appeared to offer the soundest and most satisfactory of all methods under scrutiny. Since, however, this was of a graduate order, it could not be adopted *in toto* for us at the undergraduate level. Yet the suitability, at this level, of its central and most practical feature, the employment of the 'case system' seemed quite possible if certain changes were made in the business curricula then obtaining in other and older universities. Leisurely study ripened this impression into the conviction that its adoption would enable Western to offer a type of academic training for business which would in name and principle be unique in Canada. As we looked forward down the years we had visions of the undergraduate course gradually becoming in large part or even wholly one of the graduate type, a Canadian counterpart of the Harvard course.

The recommendations of dean and registrar that an undergraduate course in business based on the 'case system' be set up at Western was approved by the Senate. The obvious steps were then promptly taken: an endeavor to secure a Canadian university graduate who was also a graduate of the Harvard School of Business, to head Western's proposed course, and pending the acquisition of such a director, the drafting by our own faculty of a provisional course for the first two years, a course designed to lead up to the introduction of the 'case method' to be employed presumably in the third and fourth years.

The provisional course was drawn up with the aid of the charted survey of all continental offerings in the field.

In the search for a director, counsel was widely sought and generously and gladly given. At Queen's, Dean O.D. Skelton guided us at once to his own university's Director of Extramural Department who had the

Dr. K.P.R. Neville (left) and Dr. W. Sherwood Fox, together, in 1919 played key roles in establishing what is now known as Western Business School – Canada's leading business school. The course in business they envisioned was based on the Harvard case method leading to a degree of Bachelor of Arts with Business Option. This picture was taken in 1947 at the time of their retirements.

qualifications required, a graduate of Queen's as well as of the Harvard Business School, Ellis H. Morrow. After an interview with him in London he was offered the directorship of the new department with the title of Professor; after due reflection upon the prospects of the situation he accepted the position. For a number of years the diploma granted each person completing the course indicated that the recipient was entitled to the degree of Bachelor of Arts in one of the two grades – either 'pass', attained after four years from admission with middle school standing, or 'honors', attained after five years from middle school or four years from upper school.

Professor, now Doctor, Morrow's success in speedily establishing firmly and on a sound basis Western's now widely recognized and, so far as Canada is concerned, unique School of Business is a distinguished achievement of which all Western men are extremely proud.

Dr. W. Sherwood Fox, President of Western from 1927-1947, although a Classics scholar, innovated the course in Business in response to the common desire of many veterans of World War I for a more formal education, of the traditional university type leading to a practical career in business.

This portrait was painted by Clare Bice, a London artist who often accompanied Dr. Fox on his outdoor jaunts and who illustrated several of his books.

# W. SHERWOOD FOX

He was a 'man of means' as wealth was described at the turn of the century and, was made the University's second Dean of Arts. He was a Classics scholar who had been educated at McMaster, Geneva and Johns Hopkins and taught Classics for six years at Princeton before coming to Western in 1917 to succeed Dr. K.P.R. Neville as head of Classics, when the latter became the Registrar of the University. Though both men were trained in the field of Classics they were of different academic origins – Neville from Queen's, Harvard and Cornell. Although diverse in backgrounds and temperaments, they remained close colleagues until the time of their retirements 30 years later.[1]

Together, in 1919, these two men played key roles in establishing what, today, is recognized as Canada's leading business school.

By 1919, the horrific World War of 1914-1918 was over. Not only had it devastated the lives of millions, but also it had had serious repercussions on institutions of learning – Western among them. The war had gradually depleted the number of students, taking some from Western and others directly from high school who would have come to college had they not enlisted. For the academic year 1915-1916 there were still 120 in Arts, of whom 80 were full-course and 40 were special students. Next year, 1916-1917, as the fighting rose in fury on the Western Front, the number of students dropped to 62, of whom 45 were full-course and 17 special students. Of these 62 students, 28 were men and 34 were women, the only period when women out-numbered men at the University.

After the end of the war, in 1919, there were 44 freshmen; an omen that attendance would increase and more faculty space would be required.[2]

Around the name of W. Sherwood Fox revolved the fortunes of The University of Western Ontario from 1917 to 1947, a period in which Western emerged from being a small, local college situated in the former Huron College building to become one of Canada's major universities on its present 1,025 acre campus site along the banks of the Thames River in London, Canada. His period began with the ordered peace and security of the late 19th century and reached across the turbulent first half of the 20th. Dr. Fox became Dean of Arts in 1919 and nine years later was installed as the University's third President. During the eventful years that followed, he was the administrative head of a struggling university that had a host of problems to be resolved – problems of finance, academic standards and those of relating the University to the Western Ontario region and establishing goodwill with local governments.

To his gift as Registrar, Dr. Neville added his efficient talents as an academic administrator. He ran, as the navy expresses it, a very tight ship. 'K.P.R.' as he was often called, though seldom to his face, was a human dynamo with a strong authoritarian streak leavened with a sense of humor. "He was," as Dr. Fox later wrote, "the perfect Registrar, a born master of filing and recording; in that field I had neither competency nor ambition. Besides, he was the master of repartee and epigram."[3] His students who remember him to this day as Dean of Arts, which he became in 1928, describe him as 'feisty'.

These sample pages are from the note-pad on which Dr. Fox wrote his recollections of events which laid the foundation for the teaching of business at Western. Written in 1958 when Dr. Fox was in his eightieth year, and troubled with failing eyesight, it provides a clear account of why he and K.P.R. Neville, in 1919, chose the Harvard case system of teaching on which to base the innovative course.

[1] & [3] Source: *Sherwood Fox of Western: Reminiscences,* by William Sherwood Fox, 1964, Toronto, Burns and MacEachern

[2] Source: *Western's First Century,* by J.R.W. Gwynne-Timothy, 1978, The University of Western Ontario

# "...Finally, the call came and I started to work in 1922"

*The Business School was built on the solid foundation designed and established by Ellis Morrow who, after six years as the first Head of Commercial Economics at Western, became known as "the real founder of our School." A graduate of Harvard Business School, he introduced the case method of teaching at Western. Following his retirement in the early 1950s from The University of British Columbia where he also established 'education for business', he candidly recalled his years at Western. This chapter, begun by him in 1954, was not completed due to his failing health.*

First word to reach me of Dean (later President) Sherwood Fox's plans to establish Business as a subject of instruction at Western came from Mr. O. D. Skelton, Dean of Arts at Queen's. As a result, I telephoned Dr. W. Sherwood Fox from Newburgh, Ontario, where I was staying with my family. This was in the summer of 1921. Dr. Fox told me over the phone that while the Business Department was in the air, no final plans had been made and to keep in touch with him.

The original plan on graduation from the Harvard Business School was for me to join the personnel department of the General Electric Company of Lynn, Massachusetts, under the direction of Mr. C. Bradley. However, the depression of 1921 had started to make itself felt at Lynn and workers were being laid off. It was, as Mr. R. B. Rice wrote me, not possible, therefore, to make new appointments to staff.

At this juncture the director of extramural courses at Queen's University resigned and Dean Skelton suggested that I should take over this work and at the same time start teaching the first courses in Industrial Management and in Marketing at Queen's. For Queen's, the fall of 1921 was an important year, because under the direction of the late Dr. Clifford W. Clark and Mr. C. E. Walker, Queen's undertook the connection with the Chartered Accountants of Ontario that lasted for so many years. At the same time, Queen's undertook to carry on educational work by bulletin and correspondence for the personnel of the chartered banks.

While the chartered accountants were automatically referred to Queen's University for their courses, a selling job had to be done in so far as the banks were concerned. Once the reorganization of the administration of the extramural courses was complete Dr. Clark suggested that I should visit the major cities of Ontario in order to meet the bank managers and their staffs and urge them to sign up for the banking courses.

I could not afford a new suit – but I could afford a new spring overcoat and hat. Thus equipped, I sallied forth and, in due course, I arrived in London and called on Dean Fox. In between bank visits I managed to meet and to discuss things with Dean Fox and Dr. K. P. R. Neville. I think the hat and coat did the trick! Dr. Harold Kingston was in London at the same time finalizing arrangements for joining the staff.

It is a long time ago and I forget the details of my talks with Dr. Fox and Dr. Neville, except that they impressed on me the great importance of sound town and gown relationships – a point which I have never lost sight of since.

At this time, London was contributing annually a substantial sum to the University and what building plans were in the air I did not know. At this time there was nothing more than discussion, but a short while later – much to the mystification of the Queen's people – I received an invitation to address the Rotary Club in London. At this luncheon I made very much the same speech as any of us would make today on the subject of Education for Business. At this time I met Mr. A. T. Little, Chairman of Western's Board, for the first time. The late Mr. Duncan McDermid of Somerville Paper Box sat along side of me and he sure was a skeptic! However, I survived eventually to enjoy his wholehearted support.

Finally the call came and I landed in London to start work on the former campus of Huron College in the fall of 1922.

---

*"Anyway, we were going to turn out, not finished businessmen, but educated men slanted to business"*

---

Problems aplenty loomed ahead and many vital decisions had to be made. Dean Fox was buried in work so he told me to work things out with the Registrar, Dr. Neville, and to report to him every now and again. The dean's stand seemed to be – "I have picked you for the job; you enjoy my confidence; go ahead and do the job."

At this time the course (undergraduate) was known as Commercial Economics (shortened to Commerce in Practice). It was a pass course (ie., three years from Senior Matriculations) and I think provided only for two courses in Accounting and two courses in Commercial Law. It was part of the Arts faculty, and the degree to be granted when there were graduates to receive it, would be Bachelor of Commerce.

Our first big advantage was that no degree in Commerce had as yet been conferred. There had been some unfortunate occurrences which had tended to make the social sciences somewhat suspect amongst the business fraternity in the City. The early problems which arose and how they were dealt with cannot be given chronological order but insofar as I remember them this was the sequence:

(1) Actually being taught were two courses in Commercial Law by Mr. F. H. Curran and two courses in Accounting by Mr. W. J. Westervelt.

(2) Expecting graduation in 1923 convocation were six men, viz: Beverly Baker, Willard C. Beamer, William J. Cowley, John Dockstader, Bruce Nimmo, and Douglas McWilliam.

(3) Behind the graduating class was a still larger class for graduation in 1924 and so on.

(4) It was decided that whatever changes would be made the University would honor its contract (implied in the calendar) with the enrolled students and that no new regulation should apply to the disadvantage of enrolled students.

(5) This resulted in a very important development, and immediate thought was given to the problem of providing the right sort of education for women going into business.

(6) The next decision was to make the course conform to Honors Arts standards and the extra year was decided on.

(7) It was decided to forget the B.Comm. idea and to award the degree of B.A. (Honors Commerce) and for the first contract years just B.A. Commerce. The reasons for this were:

(a) In a short while every university in Canada and the U.S. would be grinding out B.Comm.s and Western graduates would be identified with degrees over which we would have no control.

(b) The course was part of the Arts faculty anyway.

(c) Eventually we looked forward to graduate work and it would then not be desirable to turn out students with double standards of bachelor and master levels: (i) some bachelors would prove superior to masters; and (ii) it would only confuse prospective employers.

(d) Anyway we were going to turn out, not finished businessmen, but educated men slanted to business.

(8) Tied in with this was the decision to place men individually on the basis of a personal record carefully compiled by several members of staff so as to relieve any staff member of the invidious responsibility of recommending students to employers.

(9) It was about this time that some of the universities announced that Latin would no longer be required as a matriculation subject admitting to Commerce. This development was fully canvassed and the decision was made that Western would continue to call for Latin because:

(a) Commerce was part of Arts and should conform to Arts requirements.

(b) With the elimination of the Latin requirements, every student in the high schools would automatically head for Commerce – "No, thank you."

(c) When Arts dropped the Latin requirement it would be time enough for Commerce to do likewise.

Incidentally, some silly ass in *The London Free Press* took up this item and chased all over town asking ditch-diggers and what-have-you if they missed not having studied Latin, etc. In *The London Free Press* files of around this time you will find a big black type headline on the front page.

(10) After these policies were clarified and thoroughly canvassed by Fox, Neville and presumably by one or two key people, Neville and I tackled the problem of presenting them to the Arts faculty. It was carefully done with Fox in the chair and Neville keeping his fingers crossed.

The policies were approved not only unanimously but also with the utmost cordiality and at that moment was laid the basic success of the Commercial Course at Western. Never for a moment afterwards was I, or any of my colleagues, made to feel that we were not an indivisible part of the academic whole in the University. This is more than can be said of many other institutions.

(11) The second real break we had was the advent of Ralph Freeman as head of Economics and Political Science. Not only was he a first-class mind but also in every sense he was a helpful and co-operative colleague. As an example of this he went to Chicago for a summer in order to take Business Finance and thus equipped himself to take the finance work on the business side.

(12) Dr. Fox went to London, England, in the summer of 1924 and secured through the Kensington School of Secretarial Science, the services of a high-grade trainer, Miss Margaret Thompson, in order to establish the Secretarial School. Once again the Arts faculty wholeheartedly gave its support of the new department, once it was satisfied that the standards of the work conformed. As a matter of fact, the Secretarial Course turned out to be stiff and demanding.

That is a full history in its internal workings. The relationship with the City and with business is the other fact.

---

### "The links between Western and Harvard are basic to the success at Western."

---

The links between Western and Harvard are, I think, basic to the success at Western and account for the fact that there has been strict adherence to the case method. There is only one way to express the manner in which Dean Wallace B. Donham helped Western and that is to say with the "greatest generosity". An

illustration of this is the fact that Dean Donham, about 1925, persuaded me to ask for leave of absence for a month so as to attend the Business School as a revitalizer. He went so far as to attach me unofficially to Dr. Melvin Thomas Copeland's Bureau of Business Research so that my expenses would be all taken care of.

At this time too there was only one case book available, viz: *Marketing* by Copeland. It was, however, the time when Harvard was collecting its first cases in various phases of management and I managed to get the odd case. It was also the period when the attempt was made to establish *The Harvard Business Reports*. Why this venture did not succeed I do not know. To me it always seemed like a marvelous conception. Presumably businessmen felt they did not have time to study the reports. Another factor may have been the weight of the report volume as compared with a business journal for carrying home to read at night. Perhaps the idea could be revived in some form. *Fortune Magazine* has seemingly successfully exploited a very poor parallel of the old *Business Report;* I always felt that the *Fortune* versions left one completely unsatisfied on the essential issues – inevitable of course. At Western, of course, we had copies of the *Reports* in the library.

Incidentally I would like to make one observation regarding the case method of teaching: it is that "a case is not always necessary." After all it is simply the inductive method of teaching whereby the student is forced to find out things for himself. I always enforced one teaching rule which was "not to tell the student anything he could read or find out for himself until after he had made the attempt". It is a method of education which can be rough – but seemingly we are finding out that our educational system is too soft. It applies from top to bottom. If there is any exception it will, I think, be found in the primary schools, where the teachers are sweet and gentle in their personal relations with the pupils, but where the kids must find things out for themselves.

---

**"No university could have been in greater need of good town and gown relations."**

---

No university could have been in greater need of good town and gown relations than was Western, for the simple reason that the University was receiving direct financial support from the City of London in a big way.

The importance of this factor in the development of the institution was constantly stressed by the authorities and Dean Fox particularly devoted himself to this phase. It would have been unthinkable for the Business Department to have thought otherwise.

The problem had five phases, viz:
1. Assistance in the classroom.
2. Personal contact of staff with businessmen and their organizations.
3. Student contact with business for institutional visits, research and report work.
4. Graduate placement.
5. Adult educational classes in business.

It is difficult for me to separate my years at Western from subsequent experiences, when I was considerably better off financially (I mean personally because I never had financial assistance from an institution in this regard) and also when my children were off our hands, and we had a house suitable for entertainment.

The property purchased by the Diocese for Huron College, later the first campus of Western University, was known as "Rough Park." It stretched westward from St. George Street to the Thames River, and northward from St. James to Grosvenor Street. The college was situated in a large two-storey white brick residence, which had been formerly occupied by Lionel Ridout, an early London merchant. A dormitory wing was added to the building and a small chapel was erected on the grounds to provide for the spiritual needs of both faculty and students, and for training purposes. It was here that Ellis Morrow arrived in 1922 to head up the newly established Commercial Economics Course in Western's Arts faculty.

## "I was much influenced at Harvard by the use of visiting lecturers…"

I was much influenced at Harvard by the use of visiting lecturers in the Industrial Management group of courses under the direction of Professors Henry Farquhar and John Riegel.

This principle I transferred to Western at the level of local businessmen because I needed their help and because it heightened interest in the University.

F. H. Curran, J. W. Westervelt, C. C. Carruthers and Floyd Marshall do not come into this category as they were retained to teach specific subjects on a regular basis.

Specific comment regarding businessmen who came to speak to the students would be invidious but my general conclusions, even at Western, were that when the business visitor kept to his own operations, he was first class, informative, instructive and inspiring; but when he felt called upon to do the professional's job and tried to generalize he was a mess. This was confirmed to me over and over again in later years.

## The generosity of the London Hunt & Country Club allowed faculty to meet with businessmen.

Being 'solo' it was all up to me. Dean Fox was a member of Rotary and it was suggested to me that I might well join some other service club. I avoided the temptation for two reasons:

1. Why join one club rather than another?
2. I just simply could not stand the gaff financially. But I did become a member of the London Chamber of Commerce, then located in the Tecumseh Hotel with Mr. W. H. Wood as Manager.

I also profited from the generosity of the London Hunt & Country Club in permitting staff members to hold annual membership without having to pay initiation fees.

That tells the tale. I really met the business people at Chamber of Commerce meetings and nowhere else. But I did become well acquainted with many of the City's executives.

It was essential for students to have contact with people in business and I remember the following:

(a) Visits to various plants were surprisingly (as I look back) frequent and most of the factories were visited – Perrins, McCormicks, Empire Brass, McClary's, McHales, Holeproof, etc.

(b) Research work was very, very limited as far as I can remember. I can specifically remember only two cases, viz: *Harold Newell and Andrews Wire* (I may be wrong here) – the other case was done by Ken Totten who did a reorganization of a factory lay-out for Taylor Electric, on paper of course, but was hired after graduation to do the job on the floor.

(c) Linked with this was the hoped-for requirement that the students would work in the summer – most did. I think Allan Talbot went to Ford; Harold Newell went to Heinz at Leamington for one year and then wandered over the prairies for another year; Ken Smith worked for London Life.

## "We got a terrific opening break with graduate placement at the start."

Here we got a terrific opening break with graduate placement at the start in the spring of 1923. Largely responsible was Mr. C. H. Baird of the Bell Telephone Co. who throughout had been a friend of the department.

Whether or not Mr. Baird was responsible for the initial idea I cannot say – anyway the Bell Telephone Co. of Canada decided deliberately to hire a few University graduates in order to experiment with them and for this purpose Mr. Paul MacFarlane, the General Manager, arrived in London to inspect the crop and Mr. Baird steered him to the Business Department. In the upshot three men, Willard Beamer, Bruce Nimmo and J. A. Dockstader joined the Bell to be followed the next year by E. Cowley and J. D. Hambly. In fact the Bell became a fairly steady source of placement. Mr. St. John Haskell became the liaison officer between the company and the universities.

Of the first year's crop Bev Baker left for the U.S. as a journalist, I think; William Cowley joined Lawson & Jones in London; Douglas McWilliam secured employment with White Motors (I think by my writing to a fellow graduate who had joined the company in 1921).

Times were on the upgrade and it was easy for a few years to effect placement.

One source of placement (indirectly) was in the secondary schools of Ontario.

With a view to opening up this avenue Dean Fox and I went to Queen's Park to interview the Deputy Minister of Education, Mr. F. W. Merchant, so as to have some measure of recognition accorded our graduates after they had completed Ontario College of Education training. It was a matter of recognition for credit in business subjects for Commercial specialists. (Primarily Accounting).

B. D. NIMMO — WILLARD C. BEAMER — T. W. COWLEY — A. D. McWILLIAMS — John Dochstader — A. BEVERLEY BAKER

In 1923 these six were the first to graduate with a B.A. (Honors Commerce) from Western University. The *Western Gazette* Convocation Supplement of that year describes them as "that wild Commerce bunch" or "the Terrible Six" that formed the backbone of the Class '23.

Mr. Merchant was not overly enthusiastic, as I remember and there would have been blood on the moon had not Fox grabbed me and hustled me out to cool off. In fact I do not think we got any concession at all.

However two graduates in 1924, viz; Cyril Colwill and George Dean did not get picked up by business firms and decided that they would like to become Commercial teachers in the high schools. They went to OCE and followed their OCE year with the required training in the commercial subjects: bookkeeping, accounting, shorthand, typing, business arithmetic, etc. These two boys were a distinct shock to the educational authorities with their case training, etc. Anyway they secured the two best school jobs open in their field that year, Cyril to Galt, or Guelph, and George to Windsor.

As a result the Department of Education amended its views and Western Business graduates were accorded certain credits, but were left with the routine Commercial subjects to study after OCE.

When Margaret Thompson arrived and turned out her first crop of graduates in 1928, the gap was closed and I believe arrangements were easily effected whereby Western (still unique as far as I know) graduates from the Secretarial Course were professionally complete after their year at OCE.

This, however, belongs to the story of the Secretarial Course.

---

*"Adult education classes in Marketing were started once a week."*

---

Before Floyd Main arrived to organize and to co-ordinate the extension activities, I had made contact with the London Branch of the Commercial Travellers Association. I am not too sure, but I think that Mr. A. T. Little promoted the idea.

Anyway, under the auspices of the CTA, classes in Marketing were started once a week. Naturally the Copeland case book was the backbone of the course and instruction proceeded along orthodox lines. The classroom, I think, was the boardroom of the CTA and a tremendous protagonist of the course was Mr. George T. Hair, who was Secretary of the Branch.

Many young businessmen in London attended the class, notably, as I remember, Mr. Reg Faryon (later President of Quaker Oats) and Mr. R. E. McKillop.

The highlight of the course, however, was the tremendous support given to it by two outstanding salesmen of long success and experience. They were Mr. J. Hanna and Mr. W. T. Grant of Robinson & Little.

Before the move to the hill the arrangements for student text books were difficult. Educational books carry a low 20% discount and, therefore, can only be handled very cagily, by the regular book outlets. This is especially true of college texts and their limited purchases and insecurity of continuity of use.

In consequence Dr. Neville found it necessary to do some purchasing in order to assist the situation. He was doing this from his office in Huron College, charging full list prices and banking the funds in trust.

With the move to the hill a regular bookstore was established in the basement and Miss Elsie Pickles was put in charge. The supervision of the store operations automatically fell to the Business Department, so we set up the first accounting and stock systems. The responsibility of the funds remained with Dr. Neville whose trust fund surplus began to grow sharply.

After consultation we had arrived at the conclusion that the operation should eventually become a student co-operative; a clean surplus of at least $10,000 was necessary before a co-operative arrangement could be considered; the trust fund was just that and not part and parcel of the University consolidated accounts. (Always an argument over this point with one or two people, especially Colonel Brown. How it terminated I do not know.)

I later gathered that Hensel showed a lot of interest in developing bookstore operations.

**Editor's Note:** In 1954, Dr Morrow was too ill to continue writing these recollections. That same year, The University of Western Ontario granted him *in absentia,* a degree of Doctor of Laws, *honoris causa.* The citation is found on the following page.

## ELLIS H. MORROW

**Editor's Note:** Dr. Morrow was too ill to attend the 1954 Founders' Day Convocation. The following is the citation read on the occasion of his receiving *in absentia* a degree of Doctor of Laws, *honoris causa.*

*On this Founders' Day of March 8, 1954, as we give special recognition to the leadership which the University has given in the field of "education for business", it is natural that our thoughts should turn back to 1922 and recall the appointment of Ellis Morrow and the establishment of the academic department which, in 1950, became the School of Business Administration.*

*It was this one-time farm immigrant, Ellis Morrow, who, with his English accent and his inimitable vocabulary, introduced the case method of teaching at Western. It was this one-time Alberta school teacher who developed that significant and valuable collaboration with the Harvard Graduate Business School. It was this straight-faced, practical joker who instituted the basic philosophy that "education for business" must revolve*

*around human relations. It was this incomparable humorist, with a passion for detail, who took his responsibilities seriously but never himself. It was this friendly, lovable professor who broke up faculty meetings with his irascible wit and impressed his students and his staff with the realization that the continued strength of Canada lay in the over-all well-being of its people. He was a colorful character.*

*The School of Business Administration was built upon the solid foundation designed and laid by Professor Morrow. Today we pay tribute to him and his many contributions to the development of the University.*

*Recently retired from The University of British Columbia, where he also established a Department of Business Administration, this great, exciting and stimulating teacher, the real founder of our School of Business Administration, through ill-health, is not able to be with us on this special occasion.*

*But, Mr. Chancellor, our memories of him are vivid and our thoughts are with him as I request you, on behalf of the Senate of The University of Western Ontario, to admit,* in absentia, *Ellis Henry Morrow, to the degree of Doctor of Laws, honoris causa.*

## FROM UWO CALENDAR
### COLLEGE OF ARTS 1922-23.
Page 78-79

**Editor's Note:** To give the reader an idea of the courses taught in these early days the following are excerpts from The University of Western Ontario's Calendars:

---

**10. Elementary Accounting:** the principles underlying modern bookkeeping and accounting; books of original entry; financial statements, supporting schedules and ledger closing; single entry, double entry; business paper; synoptic and other forms of general and petty cash books; reserve and reserve funds; depreciation, amortization and sinking funds; corporation and cost records; fire loss; branch accounting; shipping and consignment, authorized trustee and executor's accounts; statements and schedules of executives administering the affairs of a manufacturing or merchandising concern, of a trustee administering matters of trust.

3 hours per week; 3 credits.

Mr. J. W. Westervelt

**20. Advanced Accounting,** auditing, accounting problems.

For all students in second year of Honor course in Commercial Economics.

3 hours per week; 3 credits.

Mr. Westervelt

**30. Commercial Law.**

1 hour per week; 1 credit.

Mr. F. H. Curran

**31. Business Organization.**

1 hour per week; 1 credit.

**32. Efficiency.**

1 hour per week; 1 credit.

**40a Principles of Advertising.**

2 hours per week, first term; 1 credit.

Mr. C. J. Bell

**41b Buying and Marketing.**

2 hours per week, second term; 1 credit.

**42a  Credits and Collections.**

2 hours per week, first term; 1 credit.

**43b  Theory and Practice of Banking.**

2 hours per week, second term; 1 credit.

Mr. Curran

# DEPARTMENT OF COMMERCE

E. H. Morrow, B.A., M.B.A.
Associate Professor

J. W. Westervelt (Jr.), C.A.
Lecturer in Accounting

D. H. Curran, B.A., LL.B.
Lecturer in Commercial Economics

C. J. Bell
Lecturer in Commercial Economics

The courses hereunder described are subject to such alterations as time and experience may make advisable. Any alterations so made, however, will not increase the requirements demanded of students who enter under the provisions of this announcement. Students who contemplate taking the Honor Course in Commercial Economics should apply to the Registrar for the special announcement covering the work in this department.

**300.  Accounting Principles:** the principles underlying modern bookkeeping and accounting; books of original entry; financial statements, supporting schedules and ledger closing; single entry, double entry; business paper, synoptic and other forms of general and petty cash books; reserve and reserve funds; depreciation, amortization and sinking funds; corporation and cost records; fire loss; branch accounting; shipping and consignment; authorized trustee and executor's accounts; statement and schedules of executives administering the affairs of a manufacturing or merchandising concern, of a trustee administering matters of trust.

3 hours per week; 3 credits.

Texts:    Cole, *Fundamentals of Accounting.*

## COLLEGE OF ARTS 1923-24.
Page 79-82

**301.  Commercial Distribution:** this course will deal with the organization and functions of marketing media; methods of marketing employed for different types of products; problems of the manufacturer and the middleman; purposes and use of credits as part of the marketing machinery; price policies; the relation of advertising to marketing problems. Problems will be assigned for intensive consideration and will be reported on in writing by the students.

During the course of the year each student will be required to submit a report embodying the methods and problems incident to the distribution of some commodity such as wheat, tobacco, rubber, etc. Particular emphasis will be attached to the Canadian phases of distribution.

2 hours per week; 2 credits.

Professor Morrow and Mr. Bell

Texts:    Duncan, Carson Samuel, *Marketing, Its Problems and Methods.*

Starch, Daniel, *Advertising.*

Copeland, Melvin Thomas, *Marketing Problems.*

Commercial and Financial Publications.

**307.  Statistics:** the chief objective of this course is to give the student an introductory knowledge of the terms, principles, forms and methods used in statistical presentation, so that he may later be able to apply this knowledge in advanced work in Commerce. The course will be divided into two sections:

I.  Theory and science of statistics

II.  The application of statistical methods to business problems

2 hours per week; 2 credits.

Professor Morrow

Texts:    King, Willford Isbell, *Elements of Statistical Method.*

Secrist, Horace, *Statistics in Business.*

**400.  Advanced Accounting:** accounting principles employed to record scientifically the transactions of a given business when extended and developed to meet conditions brought about by competition and modern methods of production and merchandising; accounts and records necessary for executorship, including points of law involving the question of personal responsibility; factory cost accounting for the determination of accurate costs entailed for material, labor and expense of designated production; partnership accounts with the law governing partners in the establishing, conduct and winding up of their business; provincial and federal enactments governing the conduct of incorporated companies and the accounts and records peculiar to joint stock companies; deferred payments or instalment accounts, adjustments rendered necessary after fire loss with the types of policies and the general contract applying to these accounts.

3 hours per week; 3 credits.

Mr. Westervelt

**401b.  Commercial Law:** this course embraces a general and particular outline of the principles of contract law from the elements to the remedies for breach; and includes special lectures on such phases of Commercial Law as agency, banking and bills of exchange, partnerships, corporations and foreign judgments.

3 hours per week for one term; 1 $\frac{1}{2}$ credits.

Mr. Curran

Texts:    Falconbridge, John Delatre, *Banking and Bills of Exchange.*

References:    Falconbridge, John Delatre, *Sales of Goods.*

Dominion and Provincial Statutes.

**402a.  Business Finance:** forms of business organization, methods of financing required in different types of organization; sources of funds for capitalization and for long term and short term financing; types of securities and legal restrictions surrounding them; relations with banks and other financial institutions; problems of financing management.

2 hours per week, first term; 1 credit.

Mr. Curran

# FROM UWO CALENDAR

**403. Marketing Problems:** the course in marketing problems is a continuation of Commerce 301. The course will be handled entirely by means of problems to be assigned once every two weeks and to be reported upon in writing. The student will be left entirely to his own resources to discover the general facts of business practice and commercial conditions bearing on each problem. It is expected that this class will be largely handled by businessmen who will assign problems within their own experience.

**404b. Finance Problems:** the course in Finance Problems will be complementary to the course in Business Finance and will illustrate the practical application of the principles learned in the first term. The course will be handled entirely by the discussion of problems that have actually occurred in the experience of business concerns and written reports will be frequently invited to lead the discussion on many of the problems submitted.

2 hoursr week, second term; 1 $^1/_2$ credits.

Mr. Curran

**405. Industrial Management:** this course will comprise a broad survey of the field of management particularly as exemplified in the management of manufacturing concerns. The first part of the session will be devoted to a discussion of the history of industrial progress and the evolution of the modern industrial plant. For this section of the course the various types of organization and the fundamental principles of management will be devoted to a consideration of specific industrial practice and of management problems in the handling of materials, equipment and personnel. Frequent exercises, problems and reports will be assigned during the course of the session. Several factory trips, for the purpose of seeing at firsthand the methods employed in different types of industry will be arranged, and the students will be required to submit reports detailing what they have seen on their trips. One report on the methods employed by a specific industry will be required during the course of the year.

2 hours per week; 3 credits.

Professor Morrow

Texts: *Principles of Industrial Management.*
Kimball, Dexter Simpson,
Assigned Readings in standard works and industrial magazines.

**501. Executive Problems:** The work taken in the various courses previous to this year will be correlated by means of written reports on problems of a general executive nature. Questions of Production, Sales and Financial Policy will have to be considered and co-ordinated in the effort to reach a solution of the problems involved. It is hoped that the problems will, in almost every instance, be assigned by an executive in some business concern. The discussions will be of a seminar rather than of a class nature.

1 hour per week; 1 credit.

**502. Applied Cost Accounting:** each student will be required to undertake a specific piece of work on cost accounting in the specialized field to which he expects to devote himself. The work must be of practical use to some business establishment, and will be done under the direct supervision of Mr. Westervelt or of some other recognized accountant. As the work will be done entirely in the field, lecture hours will be infrequent and will be largely devoted to reporting progress.

3 credits.

Mr. Westervelt

**Other Classes:** in the last year of the course the work of the students will diverge into specialized fields, the courses in which have not yet been decided upon. The classes in each case will be of an advanced character and will involve a large amount of field work. Eight credits will be given for the commerce work to be done in a student's special field. A special Commerce Announcement will later be issued, and will cover this section of the course. Those interested should apply to the Registrar for information.

Places in the classroom will be found for a limited number of men in business, who wish to avail themselves of the lectures. Anyone taking advantage of this opportunity will be expected to enroll as a special student and must secure the approval of the Registrar. Preference will be given to those having business experience.

# The move to 'the hill'

In 1924 the University moved from Huron College where it had been housed, to University College one of the first buildings to be completed on the new campus. The largest contribution to the building fund came from Middlesex County for a memorial tower to commemorate the men and women from the County who had lost their lives in the First World War. For the buildings the Board of Governors had decided on Collegiate Gothic style and all were constructed of Credit Valley limestone, quarried near Guelph. It was in the lower floor of this building the department was housed.

# "I see those wonderful years as through a golden haze."

Dr. Woonton's photograph was taken in 1977 at the time he wrote this following chapter.

*'Gar' Woonton spent his undergraduate years at Western as a Commerce student. When he registered in 1922 in the second year of the Commercial Economics Course it was an innovation on campus. He graduated as one of the 'Big Eight' in Commerce in 1925.*

*In 1977, he wrote his recollections of attending classes on the old Huron College campus.*

Occasionally, when I pass the Grosvenor apartment buildings on St. George Street, I see again, in my mind, the Huron College campus as it was when I was an undergraduate. Along with Phil Burton and Gordon Silverwood, I registered on that campus as a sophomore in the Commerce Course on a glorious day in late September, 1922. Cubby Colbert, Cyril Colwell, Ted Cowley, Les Gray and Syd Kingsmill, the other members of Arts '25 registered in Commerce, all had preceded us by one year and they were, already, old Western hands.

The University was small; it was not difficult to know everyone on the campus, at least by sight. In Commerce, Bill Beamer, Bev Baker, Bill Cowley, Johnny Dockstader and Bruce Nimmo were the seniors, all members of Arts '23. Jack Hambly, Charlie Houghtby and Ken Totten graduated in the spring of 1924.

It was not clear to me then, but it is now, that Commerce was a very new course, an innovation on the campus. The members of Arts '23 were the first ever to register and to graduate in Commerce.

The campus seemed large to me and charming, especially in the fall when the leaves were turning. Behind Huron College and at the foot of the hill, were spread out the many attractions of the semi-jungle that we called Beacher's Island (now Gibbons Park). In front, the campus bordered St. James Street and to the left, at the corner was the Bishop of Huron's Mansion (now Miss Matthew's School*) set apart by a low iron railing.

Huron College and the Faculty of Arts together formed one L-shaped building which was not young even in 1922. Huron College was the long stroke of the L and the Faculty of Arts occupied the short base. Toward St. George Street, the end of the building contained the

*Torn down and established at a new location.

residence of the principal of Huron College. Behind the building was a barn, only recently taken over from the horses by the Departments of Zoology and Physics. It was in that frigid barn under Professor W. F. Tamblyn's guidance that we struggled with Business English.

The base of the L, where the Faculty of Arts had its seven or eight rooms, was equipped with a wide verandah, mainly facing south. There we congregated in the sun, between classes or in spare hours, until the weather drove us inside to cram ourselves into a miniscule men's common room.

The principal classroom of the Department of English was sandwiched between the verandah and the common room. Whatever the season, the noise generated by our high spirits was apt to interrupt the lectures of Professor Tamblyn or Professor J. A. Spenceley. I liked and admired both of them as lecturers even though their sharp words about noise often left me much subdued.

The Annex was on St. James Street about half-way between St. George and Richmond Streets, now the site of another large apartment house. There, Miss Marjorie Ross instructed us in Library Science. There, also, I really learned to read French under the guidance of Professor Meras and his wife.

Once each week we walked the length of London to the Institute of Public Health, beside Victoria Hospital, to hear Dean H. W. Hill talk about the mysteries of the human body and its reaction to its environment. In that same building I attended lectures and did my laboratory work in Quantitative Chemical Analysis under Professor E. C. Sturdevant.

Courses requiring experts, who were not available within the Faculty of Arts, were given at an hour convenient to the expert in any room that could be found in the City. We eight Commerce students of Arts '25 met Mr. F. H. Curran (LL.B.) between 7 p.m. and 9 p.m. one evening a week, to study the Law of Contract.

That year, the meeting place was an upstairs room in the Mechanics Institute (the London Public Library, then on the southwestern corner of Queen's Avenue and Wellington Street).

Sometimes the experts came to us. Mr. J. W. Westervelt Jr. (C.A.) visited the Huron College campus two or three times each week to teach us accounting. He was a gentle, friendly man. I believe that I studied accounting with him for at least two of my three undergraduate years.

Sometimes we visited our teacher at home. Professor E. H. Morrow (M.B.A.) invited Phil Burton, Gordon Silverwood and me to take special tutoring at his residence on Maitland Street North. Those talks were not always about Commercial Economics and I suspect were as precious to the others as they were to me.

"Doc" Smith (M.D.) was the Director of Physical Education. His domain was the Western gym and Tecumseh Park. The gym was up an alley in the centre of the block

"Where the Faculty of Arts had its seven or eight rooms in the old Huron College was a wide verandah facing south. There we congregated in the sun between classes, until the weather drove us inside to cram ourselves into a miniscule men's common room."

Huron College was the site of Western University campus from 1895 to 1924. It was here that 'Gar' Woonton attended classes in Commerce. This historic building was later torn down and is where the Grosvenor apartment building is now situated.

**Garnet Woonton on graduation, 1925.**

bounded by Oxford, Colborne, Piccadilly and Waterloo Streets. Besides classes and games I remember many happy smokers and skit nights in the old gym. Rugby was practised and played in Tecumseh Park (now Labatt's Park). The team was coached by Colonel (Buster) Reid, a famous running-back in his time and a no-less famous member of Western's Board of Governors.

Besides the locale there is the epoch. I date the year 1922 by war veterans, flappers, academic gowns, automobiles, street cars and horses, but often I have difficulty believing what my mind shows me: can there have been so much technological change in so short a time?

Two unrelated events on registration day, 1922, conjure up a vision of the streets of London at that time. Outside Huron College I saw and examined a Willys-Knight (it probably belonged to Dean Sherwood Fox) with its enormous headlights (dia-acetylene burning headlights persisted into the early twenties) and all its appurtenances of luxury. As I left the campus that day, I was confronted on St. George Street by the cadaver of a horse,

killed no doubt in the course of its daily rounds while delivering bread or milk, or ice or even pulling the sprinkler used to water the dusty unpaved roads.

Academic gowns, also bring back the early twenties. Our professors always wore gowns. Many of the co-eds wore them. Huron College students probably were required to wear a gown; if it were a regulation, it certainly omitted to specify their state of repair. Of the male Arts students who wore gowns, I remember only those to whom the gown lent such a touch of distinction that with them I experienced a mild sensation of inferiority. It is my recollection that the gowns all but disappeared when we moved to the new campus in September, 1924.

By the autumn of 1922 many of the veterans of the 1914-1918 war had graduated or had left the University but there were still a few on the campus. To our generation that war was a recent world-shattering event; these veterans were our heroes. Some of them I got to know and in our talks, out of their experiences, I learned a little about life in the real world, off the campus.

Memories of initiation day flooded back thick and fast; it was rough. That day I learned that organization and planning pays off. Our seniors and betters, equipped with lengths of cord, picked us off as we entered the campus individually or in small groups. If we fought we lost most of our clothes, but our hands and sometimes our feet were bound and our faces blackened all the same. We were stored in the furnace room of the Arts wing and some of us even in the furnace itself; later we had to pay for a broken furnace. The day finished with a Roman triumph along Dundas Street; we were the chained Nubian slaves.

I admired and liked most of my professors but three stand out in my memory. I had at least one course, perhaps more, in Economics each year from Professor Ralph Freeman. His easy

style, clear statements and good humor impressed me from the first day.

Had I met Professor Fred Landon before my fourth year, I might now be an historian. He lectured to a "standing-room-only" audience in his course on American History.

On my first registration day I met Ellis Morrow, in one of his many roles, this time as Academic Counsellor. As the months and years passed, I came to know him better, perhaps intimately as we all did. He was 'Commerce at Western', the single permanent member of the University staff specifically associated with our discipline.

The University was very lucky to have found him at that critical stage in the history of the Commerce Course. He possessed the much respected M.B.A. degree from Harvard University and the mastery of his subject that went with it. He came to be respected for his good sense by his fellow faculty members and, I think, by the businessmen of Western Ontario. To us he was our friend, guide and professor.

I remember Professor Morrow as a clear, forceful and patient lecturer. Even as a young student I knew that he had drive, that he was interested in what he was doing and that he intended to do it well. I remember above all that he was a kind, understanding, human person. Two incidents may make clear what I am saying.

Once I misread the examination timetable and arrived at the appointed room just as the papers were being collected. Professor Morrow made an instant decision: he drove me to his house, gave me the paper that I had missed and told me to write at his desk. As I wrote, Mrs. Morrow, with whom I was well acquainted, brought me a substantial roast beef dinner. Perhaps I am the only student who ever passed a paper in Commerce while eating roast beef.

I was assigned to make a commercial survey of hydro-electric power in Ontario as the subject of my junior year essay. My special interests carried me away and I spent long hours in the public library working over Ontario government and other engineering reports. I was delighted with the result, but it was an amateur's engineering report and not a commercial survey. Professor Morrow read the report and treated it seriously. At the end of some hours of his time, I had learned what was needed from a commercial survey and why. Later, I spent some years making commercial surveys for the Bell Telephone Company of Canada.

I see those wonderful undergraduate years through a golden haze. Chance gave me opportunities which, nowadays, are given only to those fortunate seniors and, perhaps, juniors who are following one of the less crowded disciplines. Western was very small and the professors did not seem to be under pressure: they had time to be personal friends as well as teachers. I suspect that I learned more from them in the course of informal talks than I ever did in the lecture room.

The 1924 Executive Committee of the Commerce Club included: (back row) Garnet Woonton and Kenneth Scott, (front row) C. R. May, Edward Cowley and E. H. Morrow.

## GARNET WOONTON

Professor Emeritus Garnet Woonton died on March 24, 1980 at the age of 73. Professor Woonton was one of Canada's foremost physicists and one of the founding members of the Canadian Association of Physicists. He received his M.A. from Western in 1931 and taught at the University from 1928 to 1948. From 1955 to 1968 Professor Woonton was Chairman of the University of McGill Department of Physics and also directed the Eaton Electronics Research Laboratory at McGill. He was Director of the Centre de Recherches sur les Atomes et les Molecules at Laval University from 1971 to 1974. Western honored Professor Woonton with an honorary doctorate in 1955 and he was made a Professor Emeritus in 1977. The University's citation reads:

*To make a change in the direction of one's career is not necessarily undoing an error nor admitting to a previous uncertainty. It may be, as in the case of this former student of St. George's Public School, the London Central Collegiate, and Western University, a realization that new horizons may present greater challenges and greater opportunities. Only a man of determination and faith, possessing our honors degree in Business Administration, and with four years' experience in industry, would forsake that security of position and embark upon a new study period in the field of physics. But this man, the winner of a prize in Philosophy, did, and graduated two years later, with an M.A. in Physics, with honors.*

*Instrumental in developing our unique course in radio physics and electronics and a leader of electronic research during the war, Professor Woonton's reputation as a scientist was established and the prestige of his University enhanced...*

# Seeking the School's identity

*Lloyd Sipherd, a Harvard Business School graduate, joined Western in 1929 as one of the two professors in the Department of Business Administration, Faculty of Arts. Although he left in 1937 to go into business, he returned in 1948 and, in 1950, was appointed the first Dean of the newly established School of Business Administration. He saw the need for the School to have a separate identity and was the instigator of the move to Goodholme estate. In 1978, he wrote this chapter from his retirement home in Florida.*

Lloyd Sipherd taking part in Western's graduation ceremonies, 1957.

I arrived on the scene at Western in September of 1929. I recall that I had never been in Ontario before and when I arrived in London, I remember walking all the way out from downtown to locate the University. I was just out of the Harvard Business School and pretty green, but I was treasuring an assistant professorship with the magnanimous salary of $2,400 a year. It was my assignment to cover the courses that were taught by my predecessor, but these courses did not particularly fit into my field so I really had quite a struggle in those early days. However, having had some experience with a case method of instruction, and due to the fact there was a wonderful attitude on the part of the students, one seemed to be able to get by. However, I call your attention to the fact that there were only two of us on the faculty in that year – Philip Hensel and me. Next year, there were three when Walter Thompson came to join the faculty. This is rather interesting in that when you compare it with the total staff at the Business School now, I believe there are about 75 full-time faculty members at the School.

> ## "We had to return some of our salary to keep the University afloat."

Since it was the fall of 1929 when I reached the University, it was rather unfortunate that this really was the beginning of the big depression. I remember while we did succeed in our job, we actually did have to return some of our salary, in order to keep the University afloat, but it was something we really didn't object to. I recall many of my class of 1929 at the Harvard Business School lost their jobs within the first year or so. I felt it was rather fortunate I had chosen to enter the university teaching field instead of going directly into industry. My greatest impression of the early 1930s, which was the more serious part of the great depression, was the optimistic attitude on the part of the students. They worked hard and fortunately the enrollment of the School seemed to have held up very well. As a matter of fact, I think it increased in these years. The students appeared to have a faith in the future and demonstrated that by accepting almost any kind of job offered them, regardless of how low the salary was. The boys all worked diligently on their jobs and it is pleasant for us to note that after a number of years the boys who graduated in the early 1930s made quite a success of their business careers.

Another thing that developed around 1932 was the start of what we called graduate work. Actually it was a one-year intensive course designed primarily for Engineering graduates, who were also having difficulty finding employment in those difficult years. This was a move on the part of the Business School that really paid dividends because we had outstanding boys applying for this year of

intensive work. Consequently, we had quite a number of students leaving the University with what we called Diplomas in Business Administration to go along with their technical training.

I can recall an incident that I believe took place about 1932 that might be of interest. One of our policies was to bring outside speakers from the business world and on one occasion I remember inviting Denton Massey, who had quite a reputation for a Bible class that he was in charge of in that period, to come to the School. I remember waiting for him outside the Arts building and here he came in a Stuts convertible with the top down and wearing a coonskin coat. There were a good many students out to watch his arrival and this gave him quite a thrill, as I recall.

I left the School in January of 1937, having been invited to enter business with a close friend of mine, C. F. Wood of Hobbs Glass Co., and so I was away from school for

approximately 13 years. One of the reasons that I took this opportunity was to gain some business experience, which I really had not possessed up to that time; and I knew very well that if I ever returned to the academic field I would be much better prepared to become an instructor. Our company, Hobbs Glass Co., was acquired by Pittsburgh Plate Glass, a large American corporation, in 1949 and this gave me an opportunity to return to the University. At this very time Dr. G. Edward Hall, the University's President, and Walter Thompson were working on a plan to create a separate school of business administration, a move which certainly had the solid backing of the alumni of the School as well as the business world, and it occurred to me that this would be a wonderful opportunity for me to get back into the teaching business once again. However, this plan was somewhat sidetracked by my appointment to the first deanship of the School. I recall that during this very first year, when the Business School had been created as a separate division of the University, we were housed in the basement of the Arts building. We had to have our classes fitted into the available class room space in the Arts building and you can well imagine, it was a pretty tight squeeze. By this time the School had grown tremendously, both in the undergraduate student body as well as the graduate, and the faculty had expanded a little bit as well.

A rather unusual opportunity to move out of these cramped quarters came when the University acquired the estate known as Goodholme. This appeared to us to be an opportunity to achieve our own identity and to find better and more commodious quarters, and so we petitioned the University to move the School over to Goodholme. I remember that we were particularly fortunate in having the support of Ross Willis who was then

Goodholme, the former estate of London businessman, James Good, was purchased by the University to house the newly established School of Business Administration in 1950. The next year, operations began and the School remained in this location until 1957 when the Richard Ivey School of Business Administration Building was built on campus.

**Faculty members standing in front of Goodholme, 1952 (from left to right) Walter A. Thompson, Dwight Ladd, F.W.P. (Fred) Jones, W.R. (Bob) Waugh, Lloyd Sipherd and J.J. (Jack) Wettlaufer.**

Assistant to the President. We eventually achieved our objective.

In January, 1951, we made the move over to Goodholme. The University really went 'all out' to convert this former private residence for our use and it is interesting to note that we did have two fairly large classrooms made available to us. One, the result of flooring over the indoor swimming pool and the other, the theatre in the basement which lent itself exceedingly well to our largest classes. The living room of this house became our library and we are indebted to the University for setting up a separate library for us and providing a librarian. We obtained a faculty dining room area in what was sort of a pantry off the kitchen. The garage was converted into a snack bar for the students.

Perhaps the most valuable development was that most of the staff did get separate offices which was a luxury that we certainly did not have up to this time. The result of this

move became apparent very early in the form of a tremendous improvement in the morale, both on the part of the students and the staff.

---

*"The establishment of the Management Training Course in 1948 was a giant step forward."*

---

During the next five or six years the School was located on this separate campus and the student body continued to grow and the staff expand. For me, since I was soon to leave the deanship, this was an exceedingly interesting and inspiring period.

My career as Dean ended in 1954 and, after taking a leave of absence, I did return to the School on a part-time teaching basis until

1959, at which time I totally retired. This was a very interesting period in my teaching career and I think perhaps I did my best teaching then.

I would like to make several further observations. In particular, that in my opinion, the establishment of the Management Training Course Program in 1948 was a giant step forward for the Business School and most of the credit goes to Walter Thompson who remained as the organizer and administrator of the Management Training Course Program until his retirement recently. I believe that the performance of the faculty of the Business School in these classes, as well as several of the other new courses that have been developed since I left the School, have made a tremendous impact on the business world. It is obvious Canada now recognizes in Western a school capable of really turning out some very fine graduates.

For the past seven or eight years I have been retired to Charlottesville, Virginia where the University of Virginia is located and since I know several of the faculty here as well as the dean, I think it might be of interest to make this observation. Namely, that The University of Western Ontario's Business School is very well known here in the United States and has a very fine reputation. I think it is in order, since I have been away from the School for quite some time and have been able to observe the School from sort of 'arms length', that tremendous strides have been achieved in the development of the School, and in particular in the graduate work, where the School now has a Doctoral Program.

And, so it is with considerable pride that I point to the part which I played in the early years of the development of the Business School at The University of Western Ontario. May the School continue to expand and maintain its reputation as the finest national school of business in Canada.

MBA Graduating Class - 1956 Pictured at Goodholme

BACK ROW:      J.A. McMillan, J.A. Lovink, A.J. Roscoe, R.K. Price, R.L. Neff, L.G. Ahrens,
               P.C. Masson, R.R. Latimer, K.A. Tambling, A.K. Ham

FOURTH ROW:    J.M. MacNicol, K.M. Lindsay, W.A. Preshing, L.B. Campbell, B.E. Lanning,
               H.A. Skinner, R.N. Spilsted, T.J. Malecki, D.N. Ker, D.R. Sherk, F.W. Fitzpatrick

THIRD ROW:     G.R. Purchase, B.G. Cote, R.G. Duffy, E.N. Baker, W.J. Collett, B.H. Daniel, G. Suart,
               R.J. McLaughlin, R.W. Hardaker, C.R. Bouskill, M.H. Labbe

SECOND ROW:    R. Moreault, W.S. Kleppsattel, L.G. Ham, L.J. Richard, R.K. Ferguson (M.B.A. '58),
               D.J. Prodan, F. Panchuk, D.W. Ellis, F.D. Bush, K.F. MacDonald, W.A. Saunders

FRONT ROW:     N.M. Armstrong, John Nicholson, Miss F.E. Oxley, J.B. Washington, Lloyd W. Sipherd,
Faculty and    J.C. Taylor, Assoc. Dean Walter A. Thompson, J.J. (Jack) Wettlaufer, A.G. Huson,
Staff          David S.R. Leighton, B. Bonner

ABSENT:        Dean F.W.P. (Fred) Jones, W.R. (Bob) Waugh, R.K. Ready

# Tending the garden

*Walter A. Thompson, a man of humility, humanity and inspiration, who arrived in 1930, devoted more than 45 years to teaching leadership at the School. He looks back over those years in his roles as Acting Head of the department (1938-1942), Professor (1945-1972) and as founder and Director of the Management Training Course. He describes his contribution as that of a gardener who knows the importance of the basic efforts in producing a really good crop – which he did year after year. In this chapter, which he wrote in 1978, he recalls his years at that "very special place".*

THE 1930s

As a vegetable gardener, one knows the importance of the first efforts in producing a really good crop of vegetables; properly prepared, basic good soil, planting at the right time, good seeds, proper germination, thinning and protection of the small plants from aggressive weeds and hungry insects. When my wife, Nita, and I arrived in London in the fall of 1930, much of this important preliminary work in establishing a business program had been done. Dr. W. Sherwood Fox and Dr. K.P.R. Neville had, so very wisely, chosen Harvard[1] as a model for Western's program in business. This decision was further strengthened by choosing Ellis Morrow[2] to head the program. He was a brilliant Harvard graduate with a Queen's background and he was fortunate to have Ralph Freeman, a Rhodes Scholar and later head of Economics at Massachusetts Institute of Technology, at his elbow, as head of Western's Economics Department. During Morrow's work at Western as head of the Department of Commercial Economics, he established the case method as a basic approach to teaching management.

At one stage, faculty members from The University of Toronto, were curious and asked to come and see what Morrow was up to in his new department. In talking over the request with Dean Neville, it was decided Western faculty members would be completely open in talking about the new program – particularly about its most unusual feature – the case method. The implications of this teaching approach were completely lost on the visitors from The University of Toronto. They went away seemingly convinced that Western was involved in a 'how-to-do-it' program – a little above a technical high school activity. (A member of the Varsity faculty, 20 years later, described case teaching as "the blind leading the blind.")

Numbered notes appear on page 47.

The framework of the program when I arrived in 1930, was well underway. A most significant feature was it was an honors, not a 'pass' course. Morrow was anxious to underscore the fact that Western was not putting on a 'pass' three-year Commerce Course – with emphasis on accounting. Morrow insisted that Western's four-year honors course should lead to a Bachelor of Arts. The Western course, from the start, involved work in all phases of management including production, marketing, finance, accounting and the use of quantitative data. This is still the framework in the final two years of the undergraduate program.

The quality of students at Western, when I arrived, was another most remarkable facet of the 1930 situation. Among the men who were in the classroom with me in 1930 were such talented people as John E. Brent, who later became General Manager of IBM World Trade Corporation and President of IBM Canada; Fraser Rowland who became a Colonel and Head of the Pay Corporation in the Canadian Army during World War II; F.W.P. (Fred) Jones, President of Canadian Pittsburgh and later Dean of Western Business School; Gilbert Clarke, President of Standard Brands; Gilbert Horne, later Dean at The University of Windsor; Ross Willis who later became Vice-President, Finance, The University of Western Ontario and Acting Head of the Department of Business Administration during the war years (1942-1946); George Munro, Vice-President of Molson; Donald Wallace, who had a most interesting and exciting career with Gordon Thompson Enterprises; Stan McKay who went on to head up the marketing activities at Dupont; and Jack Brewer who was later an outstanding marketer for Continental Can.[3] These are just a few who were in my very

first classes at Western. They were followed by a host of highly talented men during the 1930s. The first graduating class was less than a dozen and by the end of the decade, the University was graduating three times this number. The numbers were not large, but the quality of student would not have been matched at many universities in 1930!

---

*"I was just 23 years-old and it was a shock to hear students call me "sir" and with a straight face."*

---

One characteristic of the Western students of the 1930s that was novel for me, an Ozark boy, was their extreme politeness. I was just 23 years-old and it was a shock to hear so many students, either older or practically my own age, call me, "sir", and with a straight face. It was wonderful that they were so polite and intelligent, because we, on the faculty, saw a great deal of each other for there were just three faculty members in the department during most of the 1930s. Lloyd Sipherd handled the Finance and Statistics Courses. Philip Hensel did the Accounting and Production Courses, while I taught Marketing, Introduction-to-Business and a Business Arithmetic Course that, secretly, I really hated. I had the students the first year in 107, the Introductory Course; 201, Marketing, during the second year; 301, Advertising during the third year; and 401, Sales Management in the fourth year. During the final year, I saw quite a few students, on a weekly basis, in connection with their thesis. No wonder I remember, so vividly, all of the people I had during the 1930s. As I look back now, those years are responsible for a host of friends I now consider my best friends. I was so lucky to have had such a group of students.

The Business Department was not highly regarded by all the members of Western's Arts and Science faculties. This attitude continued for many years. As late as 1961, a prominent faculty member vigorously opposed the School's introduction of a Ph.D Program. His reasoning was, "There wasn't enough substance to warrant a degree of this level in management." In the mid-1930s, Professor Auden, head of Classics, disapproved our proposal to grant an M.B.A. degree instead of an M.A.[4] The faculty voted our proposal down. After the negative vote, Professor H.W. Auden had a second thought, "Maybe Western's M.A. would be strengthened if we gave an M.B.A. instead of an M.A. in Business." While the Business Department, as a whole, was not regarded with great affection by some of the Arts faculty, my personal relationships with individual Arts and Science faculty were fun. As individuals, they all added up to an extremely able and effective group.

No memory of the Business School and the activities of the 1930s could be complete without mentioning Dr. Neville and Dr. Fox. These two had an idea of what quality education was all about. Through their efforts, Western was a first-class university when I arrived in London. This was accomplished with very little money. The entire University's provincial grant amounted to about as much as the University's entertainment budget 40 years later.

When we arrived, Nita, my wife, applied for a job as a cataloger. But, she was unable to work because, as a result of the depression, only one member of a family was permitted to enter the work force. She had financed my Harvard M.B.A. degree while working as a cataloger at the Massachusetts Institute of Technology. She had been the top graduate at Michigan Library School. The financial aspects of a job involving her skills at Western's library would have been exactly the same as if she had gone to work at Woolworth.

> *"When overnight expense was incurred, it was usually at Toronto's Prince George Hotel at $2 a night which we considered an extravagance."*

Travel expenses at the University were almost non-existent. One of the things we on the faculty tried to do was to give all possible help to our graduates in their search for jobs. This often involved a drive to Toronto, and back, in my old Dodge touring car, with gasoline money furnished from Nita's weekly food allowance. When overnight expense was incurred, it was usually at Toronto's Prince George Hotel at $2 a night which we considered an extravagance.

A special word should be said about Dean Neville for he was totally supportive of the business effort. So many good things happened when he was running the Arts and Science faculty. I often think of the student relations of his period and how this aspect of university life later deteriorated. He, and Helen Allison, who later became the admired Registrar in 1947, knew every student by name. Neville had a photographic memory and had almost total recall when any student, or problem, was reviewed. He had an ability for a quick comment, often a telling one, in any situation. In explaining why he disliked a particular faculty man, he told me, "he had such an irritating way of saying the obvious." Much later, after his retirement, Neville confessed it was much easier for him to "speak first and think second." He used his skills in this area to my benefit at a time when it was most needed. I have never been a model of neatness, unless

Photographed at the retirement party for F.W.P. Jones were four who, over 45 years, had led the School in its development. They include: J.J. (Jack) Wettlaufer, Fred Jones, Ross B. Willis and Walter Thompson.

one wants to point out that my habits in this area are something that a proper person should avoid. Philip Hensel, the head of our department, during most the 1930s, was the neatest man I've ever known – he used to wrap the tie he had worn during the day in tissue when it was taken off for the night. Since we in the department, all four of us including a student assistant, were in a room measuring

seven feet by six feet, my unsystematic approach must have been a real irritation to him. I'm sure this was a basic cause for his missing no opportunity to report on my many other deficiencies to Dean Neville. Dr. Neville must have viewed this as a build-up to a recommendation that Thompson should be removed from Western. Anyway, I was told years later that Dr. Neville, after hearing another complaint about me, said, "If you are about to say you want Thompson fired, you should realize this may backfire on you." The complaints stopped and next year I was promoted to Associate Professor, with no increase in pay however. Years later, I think my greatest failure as a member of the University Senate was my inability to have the names of Middlesex and Talbot buildings changed to Fox and Neville. The fact that Western has no real recognition of the contributions of these two great educators is a mystery.

I should say a bit more about the Business faculty of the 1930s. I was the low man on the faculty totem pole. Lloyd Sipherd and Philip Hensel had double pedestal desks. Hensel's status was doubly assured by a chair that allowed him to lean back and swivel – the phone at his elbow. My place in the overall pecking order was most apparent; a single pedestal desk, a straight-back chair located behind the door so when it was opened wide, and with vigor, the door handle gave the back of my chair a sharp crack. Also, the department's only filing cabinet was at my immediate right so any consultation of that important piece of equipment meant hauling and pulling of a drawer 18 inches from my right ear.

Cecil Carrothers, a London lawyer, was the oldest in age and service. He taught one class part-time in Business Law. When Carrothers couldn't come because of court appearances, he was responsible for exposing our students to some of the best London lawyers who would fill in for him on these occasions. I was lucky to have such a wise man to talk about Canadian issues during my early years.

Lloyd Sipherd was an easy man to work with. Both of us were from the mid-west. I, with a southern Missouri accent, had gone to Drury College, a small college, and then on to Harvard. Both of us were interested in athletics, he was a crack tennis player and I was fair at most sports and liked them all. He kept his

interest in the School even while he had gone, during the late 1930s, to a career in active business. When he came back later as dean he was not a stranger to the program, or to us.

Philip Hensel was one of the oddest men I've ever known. A hard worker and his teaching must have been good – he turned out men who were outstanding in accounting. Our students spent a very large amount of time on his subject – usually a good index of the effectiveness of a teacher. He was assisted in this by having one of the better students functioning as a grading assistant which allowed him to assign a great deal of written work. Lloyd and I graded our own papers (Nita took on some Business Arithmetic papers for me). Hensel's problem was his desire to live up to his salary – reputed to have been the highest at Western – $4,500. Lloyd and I, together, were making $4,900. He left suddenly in 1937 to go to Toledo University where he quite quickly became Assistant Dean. I was appointed Acting Department Head to replace him.

During the years of World War II (1939-1945) I was away from Western serving, first, as a marketing specialist with the Canadian Wartime Prices and Trade Board in Ottawa. Later, we rented our house in London and my family and I moved to Washington, D.C. where I was a senior officer in the Office of Price Administration.

---

*"While I was gone during the war years, Ross B. Willis took over as Acting Department Head."*

---

While I was gone, Ross B. Willis was appointed Acting Department Head. He did an outstanding job and later as he advanced to

senior administrative positions within the University, he remained particularly interested in the School and on more than one occasion assisted us in attaining our requirements.

In the spring of 1947, I sent the following memo to Drs. Fox and Neville and to Dr. G. Edward Hall, the newly-appointed President of Western, suggesting the establishment of a separate school for business. In addition, I pointed out the need for a special course for management training for business.

## PROGRAM TO ASSURE WESTERN'S LEADERSHIP IN THE FIELD OF BUSINESS ADMINISTRATION

1. We have an excellent background to assume this leadership.

   (a) While other schools have tended to neglect this area, we have had a more alert, balanced program.

   (b) The case approach to business study has been definitely established. We now have two courses operating wholly on our own materials.

   (c) There is a strong and loyal core of graduates in the better businesses in this country. Many, even though in their early thirties, are in top executive positions. These men have been, and will continue to be, of assistance to us in placing graduates in positions with a future, gathering case materials on business problems, undertaking miscellaneous projects in basic industrial research and educational meetings for industry.

   (d) Our *Quarterly Review of Commerce*[5] is now well established. It has been, and will be, a most useful vehicle to generally publicize the course, serve as a source of excellent material reading for the alert business executive and publicize any research we may wish to do in the future.

(e) The one year intensive course for graduates has proved to be a useful course. The soundness of the idea of giving business training to men who have specialized in a technical field has been demonstrated. This course puts us, on an enrollment basis, in the forefront in graduate work. Both McGill and Toronto engineering courses are attempting to cover this field. We will have to be alert to maintain our position. The course has consistently attracted a large number of students. During the next few years this number will naturally be greatly enhanced.

2. Other schools will establish leadership unless we take positive action. Our present leadership, if lost, is hard to regain.

(a) Toronto is establishing an Institute of Industrial Relations. A full list of courses leading to a Master of Commerce degree will be available next year. My personal contacts with staff members there indicate a great possibility for the establishment of a school of business.

(b) Cyril James (an ex-Wharton Business School man and former head of the school at McGill) will certainly see that McGill's position is strengthened.

(c) Queen's has already established itself in the field of accounting and is consolidating its position in industrial relations. A magazine similar to our *Quarterly* has just appeared. Queen's has a separate school of business.

(d) There are miscellaneous indications other universities are awakening to the possibilities of business training. The great number of veterans choosing this field is responsible for this trend. The University of British Columbia has a very large group. The University of Saskatchewan has a separate school. McMaster is starting to teach business.

3. The change of our status to that of a school will put us in a better position to become a centre of business education. Business is a professional subject and is best taught in a separate school. This is as true for business as for law, engineering, or medicine.

(a) There will be a lift in morale if a school is established here. This will be true of both staff and students. I hesitate saying this, for we are already strong on this point. Nevertheless, we can expect improvement.

(b) We will be in a more flexible position to meet the shifting problems of teaching business. The department was once turned down by the Faculty of Arts when it suggested a distinctive degree. In the future we should be in a position to deal directly with the administration.

(c) It is perceived by the general public that relative importance of courses is indicated by the status it receives within the University. Hence, I believe we will be in a better position to ask for financial support and increase our effectiveness in these areas.

1. **Distribution** – the coming problem will be in this area. We now have two important distribution scholarships and are negotiating for a third. Schools of retailing in the States are flourishing. We already teach more subjects in this field than any other Canadian school. Western graduates are sales managers of such companies as International Business Machines, Lever Brothers and Hobbs Glass. Our relations with Eaton's, Simpson's, Zeller's, Dominion Stores and other leading firms are good.

2. **Business Research** – there is no *bona fide* bureau of business research in Canada. We can probably obtain help for this project. It is on the basis of such bureaus that Harvard and other top-flight schools have established themselves.

(d) With our present status we cannot become members of the Association of Collegiate Schools of Business Administration. This membership would help us very much.

4. The establishment of the School of Business Administration should be timed for 1947-1948. It would be most dangerous to postpone the establishment beyond that

time. A later announcement would put us in the 'me too' class.

(a) I expect to be teaching at Harvard during the coming summer and will be in a better position to suggest specific plans for the School.

(b) We do not have to wait for buildings. Until it moved to its present location, Harvard Graduate School of Business Administration existed for years in the basements of Harvard Yard.

(c) While there will be some immediate increase in costs, these increases can be kept at a reasonable figure. We will be in a better position to actively solicit support from industry for research, fellowships, the teaching of specific subjects and buildings.

I thought this memo had convinced Dr. Hall of the need to establish a separate school as well as a special management training course for business. When no action was taken, we on faculty tried to think of the proper approach to make things happen. When the idea was broached of offering to hand in our resignations if it was felt the status of the department was not up to 'School' level, one member objected. He suggested we might be allowed to resign. It was with this as background, I approached Fred Jones to have alumni pressure brought to bear on the administration. Fred, together with London businessmen Gordon Silverwood and Harold Newell, who had obtained a B.A. degree at Western in 1927 and was now with Andrews Wire Works in Watford, Ontario, were able to convince him because in 1947, at fall gatherings of business graduates, he made the statement that the department should become a separate school.

---

**"Dr. Hall had the idea, in the spring of 1948 of our holding a meeting with management people."**

---

Dr. Hall had the idea, in the spring of 1948, of our holding a meeting with Canadian management people to ask them the question, "What should Western be doing now in the area of management?" It was hoped that the answer would include the establishment of a school of business administration. To assist in this project, a meeting of Canadian executives was called together in London to consider education for executive responsibility in business. This was under the planning and chairmanship of Robert (Bob) Reid, President of the London Life Insurance Company. One of the actions growing out of this meeting was the setting up of a group of businessmen to advise on academic policy. This group was headed by Lloyd Sipherd, Vice-President of Hobbs Glass, and included Larry Dampier, Director of Sales, Lever Brothers, A.J. Little who was a partner with the accounting firm Clarkson Gordon, Harold Newell, President, Andrews Wire Works.

Invitations signed by Bob Reid were sent out to the appropriate group of senior managers in the spring of 1948. Much to our amazement, Room 30 of the old Arts building was nearly filled that April afternoon. There was never a less structured meeting. Bob Reid chaired the gathering and underscored the importance of the purpose of the meeting. I outlined what we were doing at Western in management education and the discussion from the floor took over.

N.R. ('Buck') Crump who was Vice-President, and later President of Canadian Pacific Railway, stated his view that education in this area was a big job and should reach down into organizations, not just the top of the organization. There was wide acceptance of the idea that Canada should have a university with a management program of a quality that would compare favorably with any other school anywhere.

I can still visualize J.R. White, Vice-President, and later President, of Imperial Oil saying we should certainly have a short course for practicing managers similar to Harvard's Advanced Management Program. The line of reasoning was that business, generally, had put itself in a vicarious position in its ability to have people ready to take on senior management responsibility. This was partly due to the stagnation of the depression[6], when the idea that without anyone doing anything, cream would rise to the top. It was also felt talented people in the organization required no special attention. The prevailing school of thought was that the 'get-ahead person' in an organization, willy nilly, got to know the job of the man ahead of him. These two approaches to developing managers were supposed to take care of the need for management people. The Second World War had prevented even these antique approaches from working. One person expressed the problem this way – "We have men in district offices that are OK there, but we are scared to bring them into head office." The meeting had struck a subject that had high priority in the minds of people who were responsible for running Canadian business.

The meeting could not have ended in a more satisfactory way for Western. There was a consensus on four points:

1. Western should have a respectable school, emphasizing graduate work;
2. there should be a short course for experienced managers;
3. business was willing to put money into the venture; and
4. there was to be a committee of business people to assist in all these things.

The consensus was that there should be an immediate meeting of a small group of business people to meet with Western staff and implement their ideas.[7] It was at this later meeting at The University Club in Toronto that I agreed to organize a course, in the summer of 1948 for senior managers. I didn't know at that moment all the things that would have to be done before the first class arrived at the old Huron College campus one hot afternoon in August. Becoming operational in setting up the course was not easy. We had no budget. However, Gordon Thompson, one of Canada's most talented entrepreneurs and a highly interested board member, was very helpful. He told me to go ahead and put on the best course I knew how and not to worry about how much it cost.

The first move was to go to 'head office' (Harvard) for help.[8] Fortunately, I had spent the previous summer at Harvard as a visiting professor. At that time, I renewed personal friendships and brought myself up to date on Harvard's post-war thinking. Much had been going on in management education and this gave me the opportunity to review the best thinking in this area of education. My four years away from Western during the war years were spent on matters totally unrelated to teaching. There were two men in particular at Harvard with whom I wanted to talk to about our situation – Stanley Teale who was Dean of the Business School and an old Harvard classmate, and Ed Learned, one of the really great Harvard professors. Stan, when I told him my problem, asked, "What do you want to know, the big things about our Advanced Management Course or the little things that make it work?" He told me both. It was obvious we couldn't do in four weeks what Harvard did

in 18. However, we could give a good exposure to one of Harvard's really great post-war innovations: its revolutionary course in 'Administrative Practices'. Ed Learned suggested Ralph Hower would do a good job for us. Ralph, happily agreed to come for the four weeks.[9] We have never worked any professor on any program harder. He had two classes on Monday, one on Tuesday, Wednesday and Thursday and two again on Friday, for four weeks. He did an absolutely superb job for us.

This course was a real 'leap forward' in the teaching of management. The Harvard 'Ad Prac' Course was teaching concepts that the pedestrian academics in other universities came to 20 years later. The 'Administrative Practices' Course was an exciting and exhilarating experience for early Management Training Course class members. Many said, "My boss simply must take this course."

---

### "'Ad Prac' was the heart of the early Management Training Course courses."

---

'Ad Prac' was given full treatment and was the heart of the early Management Training Course courses. Lloyd Sipherd, later to be our first Dean, joined us in our first discussion of the overall course content. I believe it was Lloyd who suggested we use the non-'Ad Prac' time for discussing the most interesting and important cases in the other fields – marketing, finance, production and accounting. All of these formed a course in policy. Graydon Jarmain came up with the name of the course. In his practical way, he suggested that since this was a course for training managers, why not call it what it was, "The Management Training Course."[10]

As time went on, there were naturally changes in course content. A week was added when almost every member of the first course said it was "too short." This complaint was taken later to mean they really liked the course. This extra week gave us a little more elbow room. Later, we got a little extra time by adding Saturday classes and shortening the 'long weekend' by a day. This long weekend had been inserted to give the men a break from the heavy grind that they had subjected themselves to. An addition of more weeks was often discussed with the Advisory Committee but the overall length has remained at five weeks.

The materials added to later courses reflected the development in the teaching of management as well as to the additions to our faculty. Labor Relations was introduced and was taught by Jack Wettlaufer, who had been working closely with Ben Selekman of Harvard. Jack's series on labor has been immensely successful. The students always have a 'live' case with him. There is always a major strike on or about to happen, and he brings this case to the classroom. Business Policy, as a course, was added, reflecting the maturing of this course in our regular curriculum. Charles Bliss of Harvard carried the brunt of activity in the early stages and Donald H. Thain of our faculty, later. Don, along with Jack teaching in the last weeks of the course, have always given the class members a lift, at a time when it has been needed.

The use of the computer in decision making came into being after 1948. Andrew Grindlay, and our staff, established this course. Donald Thain later introduced his course in Business and Government. Accounting presented an interesting teaching problem. As the course developed, it was evident that many didn't know much about the quantitative side of management – and a large number of class periods were always set aside for this activity.

Since the class also had a large number of expert accountants, there was a problem of what to do with these people while the bulk of the class members were being initiated into the primitive aspects of accounting. Bob Taylor, who with Harvard's Ross Walker, handled this area in the early courses, excused these men from the class during the early sessions. Later, it was decided that these men should stay in the classroom as observers and learn how an expert brings along total greenhorns to know something of the mysteries of accounting. By watching Bob Taylor and Ross Walker do this, they were getting excellent teaching hints. They were also asked to act as resource people in study groups.

Further help to non-accountants was given by having extra sessions[11] in the afternoon and by sending out materials dealing with accounting vocabulary before the course started. Since the men on the course were key people with heavy regular workloads, particularly when getting ready to leave the office and home for five weeks, we felt it unrealistic to intrude in this busy period just before leaving for London. So, as a rule, little pre-course material was sent.

**Walter in the classroom with members of the 1978 Management Training Course. Over the years, a number of MTC graduates have said, "It was the most significant experience of my life."**

## OBJECTIVES OF THE MANAGEMENT TRAINING COURSE

When Queen Victoria was told she was to be Queen of England, her first words were, "I will be good." This was Charlie Bliss's example of primitive planning. He quoted her as he started the section of Business Policy that dealt with planning. I have already referred to Gordon Thompson's advice "disregard costs as you plan the course – just do the best course possible."

The top management people told us of their need to establish a general management point-of-view in their specialized people. Most firms had people who had spent their careers being better at production, marketing, etc. They were good at their existing job – a specialized one, but were deficient when brought up to do a general management job. Edgar Burton, President of Simpson's, who I had known during the war while working with the Wartime Prices and Trade Board – gave me most useful advice, "I don't want the course participant I send to you to learn anything about such things as store layout and the technical side of his or her job. What participants need help with is learning how to deal with people." As a result, general management and peoples' points-of-view were always in front of us as we developed the course content for the Management Training Course.

Very soon after the course was introduced, each manager who sent a participant to the course was asked to tell, in a confidential letter to me, his idea of the strengths and weaknesses of his employee. I was particularly interested in the weaknesses. Year after year, the 'people weaknesses' were emphasized. Lack of knowledge of areas other than that of the employee's specialization was very frequently mentioned. Contacts with those who had taken the course, both personally and by letter, indicated they had received a host of helpful benefits. A number have said to me it

was "the most significant experience of my life." In many ways, the course was designed to make available a 'cafeteria' where participants could get help with their own unique problems. The over-confident were regularly cut down to size in a heated discussion of a case. The man who was too quick to make a decision was slowed down.

On the other hand, there were class members from smaller corporations who had made their way to senior jobs and weren't sure of themselves. The rough and tumble of banging away at case problems gave them confidence – they were able to hold their own against men from highly respected corporations. One such man told me, "I never knew if I got my promotion to my job because I was liked by the owner and just happened to be around, or whether I deserved my promotion." He found he could hold his own in competition with the good men in the classroom. One wise man told me the self-evaluation effect of a good training program is one of the greatest benefits. A lot of introspection has always gone on in the Management Training Course.

The use of actual management cases is an excellent tool in teaching. The five weeks duration of the course allows for the acquisition of much experience. During this time class members experience, in depth, about 90 important management problems. The speed with which this experience accumulates was driven home to me after I discussed a marketing case involving the Imperial Furniture Company. The case dealt with the company's post-war strategy. Howard Hemphill and Donald Strudely, the senior executives of the firm, sat in the class and heard the discussion of the problems. Their identity was not known to the class until I asked them, at the end of the hour, to comment on what they

had heard. Their statement was that the class, in an hour and 10 minutes, touched on every bit of thinking it had taken them two years to consider. When 90 problems are diagnosed and conclusions regarding the actions to be taken are discussed over five weeks, the class members have absorbed a great deal of insight. Carlton Williams, when President of the University, at one of the final day exercises told the class, "Whether you know it or not, you will never be the same."

Ross Walker, in talking about what the Management Training Course was all about, spoke of it as an experience that should rid the class member of a lot of 'dead horses' – these dead horses being old and outworn management clichés that no longer, if ever, worked. Arthur Sutherland, an early class member and later President of Shawinigan Chemicals, referred to this in a talk he gave at the final exercise of a later class. He said, "When the boss has dead horses, they breed." Ross Walker also used to talk about the course enabling the man to "shift gears."

From a pretty realistic point of view, a major goal of the course has been to sharpen decision making and decision implementation. The participants on the course are in a stage of their careers which has moved them away from the lower management levels. In their early years, management policy and precedent are important, and as managers they are close to what is happening. This being true, errors can be quickly spotted and corrected with major, or slight shifts in decisions. As they move up, the decisions are much more important. Their position is less and less structured and a larger number of variables are in the situation. They know less and less about the whole situation on an 'eyeball-to-eyeball' basis. The Management Training Course was designed to help managers through this transition period.

> *"We were told it was in small study groups class members were getting their greatest benefits."*

Having organized small study groups is one aspect of management courses that Western can claim. In the early days, we were constantly being told it was in small groups, studying for the next day's cases, that class members were getting their greatest benefits. This was hardly a flattering statement to a faculty teacher whose ego was at a high level by having the most satisfying classes he had ever experienced. We finally decided, even if only just to maintain our dignity, to institute organized small study groups. It was quickly apparent that this was a most useful tool. A really good discussion of a case in the large classroom will result in approximately 30 contributions – I have counted this many times. In a study group of from 10 to 12 and lasting 45 minutes, everyone gets in on the discussion. This takes away some of the frustration of a class member not being able to contribute to the large class discussion. The less-aggressive individual often found his pearl being cast by a more vigorous classmate.[12]

It was in the smaller groups that hair was really taken down. This aspect of the whole operation was of tremendous value. Jack Wettlaufer used to calculate the total years of management experience that existed in the typical class. With the average age running about 42 years – and the men in all kinds of management jobs everywhere – there was regularly at least 2,000 years of management experience in the typical classroom. The sharing of this invaluable commodity was going on all the time during the five weeks – the transfer of experience was usually at its peak in the small study groups.

The faculty consensus was that the effectiveness of the average class jumped at least 15% after this innovation became operational. One of the greatest time savers was the sorting out of technical terms – clearing out misconceptions – really zeroing in on the important problems and brushing aside the unproductive contributions that get in the way of a group of people really getting at the important problems. The faculty teacher was helped too. If there was a mechanical error in the case material, he found out about it and corrected the matter. He could see during his brief visits to the 10 to 12 small groups how the class was reacting to materials and this helped shape his next day's strategy. His visits underscored our message to the class that study

# Canadians Visit Harvard to Study Business School

**Boston, Mass.** (Staff).—Board of governors and leading members of the faculty of the University of Western Ontario, on Friday, were given an intensive inside view of all that makes Harvard University graduate school of business administration tick. Arriving by plane and train, the visitors were shown over the administration buildings, dormitories, lecture rooms, business library and various halls.

**In conferences,** morning and afternoon, Associate Dean Stanley F. Teele fully explained the general objectives of the school and called on Dean Harvey P. Bishop, Prof. Ralph M. Hower, Prof. Franklin E. Folts, Mr. Arthur H. Tully and Prof. James W. Culliton to explain and answer questions concerning the Advance management program, the MBA program, the associates and research and the case method.

**On the delegation,** leading Canadian businessmen included: J. H. Barth, Windsor; W. H. Clark of the Ford Company, Windsor; Arthur Ford, chancellor UWO, London; L. R. Gray, London; D. B. Greig, Windsor; Dr. G. E. Hall, president UWO; J. B. Hay, London; P. R. Hillborn, Waterloo; G. J. Ingram, London; R. G. Ivey, chairman of the governor's committee on the UWO Business School, London; A. J. Little, Toronto; H. A. MacKenzie, London; A. E. Pequegnat, Waterloo; G. H. Sheppard, president IBM of Canada, Toronto; J. R. White, vice-president Imperial Oil, Toronto; C. F. Wood, president Hobbs Glass, Ltd., Toronto; Walter J. Blackburn, president London Free Press Co.; Dean L. W. Cipherd and Associate Dean W. A. Thompson of the UWO Business School, London. Two business school committees were represented among the visitors, one headed by Mr. Ivey and the other an academic advisory committee headed by A. J. Little.

**P Three Canadians** attending the Business School of Harvard were present at conferences to answer any questions by vistiors on the students' views as to the value of the courses. These were C. Alex Manson, Sales manager of the B. C. Electric Railway Co., who found the advanced management program very stimulating; Ernest C. Dancher, a UWO graduate, and Douglas C. Matthews, a University of Toronto graduate.

*The Globe and Mail,* Monday, May 15, 1950

groups were important. It was hard during the professor's visits not to hop into the discussion – but the faculty had to keep a 'hands off' approach to this aspect of the course. Study groups were the responsibility of the class members. The role of the chairman puzzled a lot of people. They were told the role was really that of a traffic cop. It was not possible in the short time available to come up with a case solution. It was good to drive for a consensus. The actual membership of each group was a random affair. In the early years, when making up the study groups each course member's name was on a card – different colors to relieve the monotony! These were shuffled and dealt into 12 piles, three times daily. The advent of the computer eventually took care of this time consuming occupation. During the early part of the course, the groups were frozen. After three days, a new group was formed for each case. Later, a group would do all the preparation for the three cases next day. This was a marvelous way for every class member to work intensively with everyone in the course. When one works with another person, one really gets to know him. One of the really great pluses of the whole experience is the acquisition of so large a number of wonderful friends.[13] Someone has said that one of the basic meanings of the word love is to know a person. Love is certainly an important aspect of the Management Training Course. Study groups have a large part in making this possible.

---

*"The first classes were fed in Fingal Hall, an old airforce building the University had acquired to help cope with the post-war lack of facilities."*

---

The straight-jacket of work imposed by the schedule was tough. To achieve the objectives of the course made hard work absolutely necessary. It was up to us to make the

necessary work load livable. The residence on the old Huron College campus gave us our bedrooms and dining hall. The old Huron was really something! One class member told me that during his army days he had slept on some hard beds. None of these, he felt, could compare with the hardness of the beds we had in the old Huron. The class seats were hard too, and seat pads were added during the second year of the course.

The Management Training Course owes a great deal to Huron College and Harry O'Neil for the wonderful way they helped to make the early sessions of the Management Training Course so useful. It was not without regret that we moved from Huron College to the tailor-made facilities of Medway Hall.

The first classes were fed in Fingal Hall, an old airforce building the University had moved up from Fingal, Ontario, to help cope with the post-war lack of facilities. It was called Fungus Hall by students. George Bullas even brought in 300 blocks of ice and put electric fans behind them in his attempt to make the dining room more livable during a particularly hot day.

The cooks at the old Huron were used to meeting budgets that did not allow for the use of such things as butter. It took them a little while to get used to the idea that we wanted to pay for the best. Huron was so spartan that we tried to make up for it in other ways. The London Hunt Club generously made membership available to us at a very moderate fee. The London Club followed, and the YMCA helped. As our facilities at Western improved, these facilities were not as necessary. The Hunt Club moved to its new location and golf receded as an important aspect of the whole affair. London businessmen and friends of the University went all out in the early days to make our men welcome to London. There were at least two cocktail parties each weekend. It soon became

apparent that this was too much and this was cut to two for the whole course. One was given by the president of the University at the end of the first week and a second during the latter period by the chairman of the board.

The 'out-of-class' activities were pretty much under the control of the participants themselves. We encouraged a speedy election of a class executive which took over much of the essential extra curricular activities. Many of these were done with the flair of top professionals. This was demonstrated when R.W. (Bob) Southam, Publisher of *The Ottawa Citizen* and Ross Munro, distinguished war correspondent and Editor of *The Vancouver Daily Province*, put out their year book[14] called *LIFO* – a beautiful copy of a *LIFE* style magazine with the format adjusted to the Management Training Course. As the men got to really know each other and realized, during the latter stages of the course, that all this was coming to an end, the socializing after the 10 o'clock snack became intense, and at times dysfunctional.

The final socializing at the end of the course was a fun event. The last night started as a stag affair. The entertainment was usually pretty wonderful. All sorts of talents were discovered. One theater buff put on a sequence of really great skits at the new Hunt Club's dining room. I had some anxious moments when a skit involved a Roman scene. One of the characters came in dressed in a toga carrying a torch. Unfortunately, the torch was smoking heavily. For a little while I was trying to estimate the size of the bill we would surely be getting from the Hunt Club for the blackened ceiling in their beautiful, brand-new dining room. Luckily, no visible damage was produced.

Much later, when the course was housed in the new Huron College, the class members returned to their rooms after a vigorous final stag party to find every room completely bare of any furniture. They were very tired and ready to go to bed. John Metras' football players, who had arrived a few days earlier for fall practice, had moved into another part of the dormitory. They thought it would be fun to move all the furniture to the attic. After a suitable interval, the whole squad of huskies came to our rescue and helped move all of it back.

The final day exercises have always been memorable. After the presentation of diplomas, George Bullas and his staff came through with a superb luncheon. This was attended by wives, children, relatives, bosses and business associates. The large dining hall at Somerville was always full. It was always such a pleasure to see the wives, and later the stag was replaced by a husband-wife party. The party, arranged to mark my retirement from the Management Training Course after 25 years, was a highlight and this, and previous such affairs, proved to me that one of the necessities of being a successful manager was boundless energy.

Angela Challenor, who joined us in the summer of 1954, was a mighty factor in seeing that all went well during the course. Teaching and other activities claimed much of my time during the winter and the 'getting ready' period of the operations. In other universities, heading up a similar course was considered to be a full-time year-round job but this was not the case at Western. Her eye for detail and ability to memorize the names and occupations of all the class members (including those who attended before her time) was a great asset. She remained with the course until 1971.

In the early days, Barbara and Bob Waugh saw to it the class had teaching materials in place. We had some tight squeaks particularly the Saturday before the first class. The entire faculty, and all the Thompson family, followed each other around tables collating mimeographed materials. Bob Waugh was often putting the materials in the class members' rooms as they were checking into the dormitory. This was a much tougher job before copying machines, and hundreds of stencils

had to be typed. Neil Armstrong, with his desire to have things just right, helped very much. The little things that Dean Teale had in mind to make programs go were well taken care of at Western.

We have had meetings of personnel people to discuss programs for management people. A great number of these personnel managers have been puzzled over why the Management Training Course always went so well. The physical facilities at the outset were somewhat primitive. We ended, of course, with a nearly perfect situation on this phase of our activities. The most important element was having the kind of class members we had – talented, experienced persons in management with their companies backing them and who wanted to improve their management skills and were willing to pay a high price in terms of effort to make real progress in the effort.[15] The big price was five weeks of strenuous work. The program was designed for maximum drawing on the experience of each one in the class.[16] From my point of view, the instant feedback of the group on matters that would get in the way of the success of the course was invaluable. Before we had our first course, Harvey Bishop, who was managing Harvard's Advanced Management Program, told me of the importance of constant contact with the class to make it easier to get this information. I sometimes feel that I'm overly pollyannish when I verbalize on the quality and lovability of all these past Management Training Course members. They were at the core of the good things that happened.

The faculty has always been tremendous. With the exception of the Harvard people, no one knew what, if anything, they would be paid for their work on the first course. It has always been a labor of love – fortunately, later courses have involved a trip to the bank for Western people. The Harvard group was always superb. The opportunity of Western faculty to

work with, and profit by, the intimate contacts made available through the course contributed so much to all of our development as teachers. Gradually, I heard more and more, "Why do you bring in Harvard people when you have such superb men as Wettlaufer, Taylor, Thain, Leighton, Hodgson, etc.?" This group never regarded the time in the classroom as their sole job – previous and past course work was done well. While the course was on, they were constantly with the group, at meals, snacks, sports. Class pictures and biographies were carefully studied before the course started – so many were recognized at first sight. Jim Taylor was particularly good at this – so was Dwight Ladd. The contribution of the faculty wives should not go unmentioned. They used to put on the reception that was held on the first Sunday afternoon. We, later, were able to have it catered by the Food Services Department. Wives gave up seeing much of their husbands during those five weeks.

I was involved from breakfast to the 10 p.m. snack. While the time commitment for both class members and faculty was intense, it was great fun[17] to participate in the Management Training Course.

EPILOGUE

Although Walter wrote his recollections in 1988, he asked to see the proofs for this book in 1993. He, now 86, and Nita, 89, were cozily living in the home on Richmond Street they had occupied for over 50 years.

After Walter had read his piece, he commented, "I have left out so much. Perhaps, I could sum up by saying Western Business School is a very special place. It is different from other institutions of learning in the quality of its leadership and the excellence and diversity of its faculty, student body and caring alumni. I am so happy I was part of it and only wish, with the coming of a new year I had a new crop of students to tend."

## WALTER ALBERT THOMPSON

received honorary degrees from Wilfred Laurier, York University, Bishops, and from his alma mater Drury College in Springfield, Missouri.

On June 6, 1973 Dr. D. Carlton Williams, President and Vice-Chancellor at The University of Western Ontario delivered the following citation:

*He arrived on the Western campus in the fall of 1930 at the ripe age of twenty-three after graduating from Drury College and the Harvard Business School. With the exception of the war years, he has been here ever since.*

*Over those years, no individual has done more than this native of Missouri to help Western's School of Business Administration achieve its international reputation. While from the first, he wrote cases, did research and engaged in consulting activities, his main impact on the generations of devoted students who have passed through his hands, has been as teacher, counsellor and friend. The evidence is not hard to find. How many professors get 'evaluated' by being presented first with a new car\*, and then, on retirement, with a Fellowship Fund in their name in an amount sufficient annually to provide three $1,000 Fellowships?*

*During the war years he was in turn a marketing specialist with the Canadian Wartime Prices and Trade Board and a senior officer of the Office of Price Administration in Washington. Shortly after his return to Western he organized and ran for twenty-five years his widely-acclaimed management development course, a program whose only possible rival is the course in advanced management at Harvard.*

*Five years ago he became interested in the Caribbean. With the financial backing of the Canadian International Development Agency, Walter Thompson is working actively with the University of the West Indies to help develop management studies on its campuses in Jamaica and Trinidad.*

*Lest the erroneous opinion be formed that his only exercise consists of walking on water, it must also be recorded that he can be amiably stubborn as well as exquisitely absent-minded. For example, despite the fact that three of his children are champion swimmers, Walter Thompson cannot and will not swim. To show what they think of this obstinate refusal to learn, the Business School faculty has donated the Walter A. Thompson trophy to be awarded annually to the best swimmer in the freshman class. Again, to outwit his uncanny propensity to misplace important documents, they made sure that their gift of return tickets to Europe was addressed and handed to Mrs. Thompson.*

*Walter Thompson's interest in The University of Western Ontario has extended well beyond the confines of the Business School. He was a member of its Senate for many years, and was one of that first group of four faculty Senators to be elected to the Board of Governors.*

*Mr. Chancellor, in the name of the Senate I ask you to confer the degree of Doctor of Laws, honoris causa, on Walter Albert Thompson, Canada's foremost business teacher and Western's pride. He finds nothing incongruous in combining gentleness of manner with blunt forthright honesty. Similarly his determination to build a great institution has never interfered with his ability to find time for individuals. Nor does he see any incongruity in loyally serving Canada for forty years and raising two generations of Canadian offspring, while remaining himself a card-carrying American! If this be the American invasion of Canadian universities, long may it flourish!*

---

\*In 1955, to mark Walter Thompson's 25th anniversary at the School, a group of his admirers, headed by D.D.C. (Don) McGeachy (Diploma in Business Administration '46) and Professor Jim Taylor, decided to present him with a new car – a possession he had never had.

Don McGeachy, in recalling the circumstances leading up to the gift, said, "We felt Walter had never received the recognition he deserved and we wanted to pay tribute to him while at the same time sending a clear message to the University of Walter's great contribution to business education. We were uncertain as to the response we would receive from alumni and friends on asking for donations so I said I would underwrite the purchase of a, well, modest car. Jim and I sent out letters asking for funds. They came pouring in! We were able to buy a top-of-the-line, black Chrysler Newport with all the trimmings. When we gave it to Walter, at a party arranged in his honor, he was astonished and even more so when we gave him a cheque for the thousand dollars left over after the car had been paid for. In his inimitable way, Walter promptly turned it over to the School's library. Later, I heard from the chairman of the Board of Governors, the University had received the message."

# 'Walterisms revisited' – NOTES

[1] Harvard's continued assistance and influence to the Business School through the years is a wonderful example of generosity. We relied wholly on them for our staff replacements for many years. A wealth of examples of this help will be found in this record of the development of the School. Some measure of Western's realization of Harvard's assistance is indicated by the fact Western has awarded six Honorary Doctorates to Harvard Business School faculty: Deans Donald David; Stanley Teale; George Baker and Professors Franklin Folts and Ross Walker. More recently, the current dean, John McArthur was awarded an honorary degree.

[2] Ellis Morrow was a wonderful man, an English immigrant, a constable in his youth who married a school teacher. She decided he should go to college – which sent him, in his late twenties, to Queen's University. After graduation, he stayed on there where he was involved in publications. He then went on to Harvard where he achieved an excellent academic record.

[3] It is so dangerous to mention names at all, one is always omitting persons that should be mentioned. I can think of three right now which should have been included. I will not add their names so all who are left out will know they are among the three.

[4] Professor Auden used to refer to the Business Department as "Westervelt on the Hill" – Westervelt being a for-profit business college downtown that specialized in turning out stenographers.

[5] Name changed to *The Business Quarterly* in 1950

[6] Ogilvie of CIL said that they didn't really go out to get high talent people during the depression – those they got left them.

[7] The group met at The University Club in Toronto and included, among others, Douglas Grieg, President of Ford, who agreed to chair the effort. A.J. ('Pete') Little, a Western graduate and a Clarkson Gordon partner, Bob Reid of London Life, Jack White, President of Imperial Oil, and Hugh Mackenzie, Vice-President and General Manager of John Labatt Limited.

[8] I have been a follower of Descartes in my approach to problems. He believed that he should not do anything without thinking it through. After making this decision, he realized he couldn't take his next breath – there wasn't time. As an operational rule, he decided that, pending the availability of time, he would choose someone he admired and do as he did until he got around to thinking through everything. We were later criticized by a professor who visited us on his way to Vancouver to take up the headship of the program at The University of British Columbia. He said, "We didn't do enough of our own thinking."

[9] Ed Learned headed this teaching group in 1948. The whole idea was started with Harvard's marvelous innovator, Dean Wallace Donham. Upon his retirement as Dean, he really got involved in this course. He said that Harvard had misnamed its school, The Harvard School of Business Administration. He said it should have been called a School in Decision Making. The new course involved the administration of decisions, without worrying too much about the logics of the actual decision. The teaching group that was brought together included Ed Learned, Fritz Roethli, S. Berger, Jack Glover, Ralph Hower and Ken Anderes. It was really remarkable.

[10] London people were generous with their weekend entertaining of the class. One Saturday at Arthur Little's, Western's Chairman of the Board at that time, a party was given for the class. One of the local businessmen, who knew little of the purpose of the course, saw Fred Palin, then General Manager and later President of Union Gas. He was puzzled by his attending the course and asked, "Why is Palin here? He is already a success."

[11] We regularly avoided special courses for special interests. We wanted to keep the whole group as a group. Commonalty of experience, we felt, was essential to the group's wholeness. We, unsuccessfully, introduced sensitivity group sessions as an extra. This was abandoned after one try. Columbia in their Senior Managers' Course, had this activity as an integral part of the whole session. The results, as reported to me by Hoke Simpson, who headed this area, were total chaos, and a lot of anger among the men and the faculty.

[12] The shift in the type of person coming in on the class discussion was interesting. The 'sales types' were the early, heavy participants. As the days went by, under the steady pressure – often very thoughtful persons became more prominent.

[13] The best demonstration I can think of this is what happened to the class of 1952. This group has met dozens of times in Montreal, Toronto, Kitchener, London and Ottawa. At their 25th reunion, half the original class attended. Many of their gatherings have not been just fun. I have heard some of the most insightful discussions of important problems at their get-togethers.

[14] Several years later I ran into Frank Sherk – then President of Heinz, and we were talking about some people who were in his class. He reached down to his briefcase and fished out his year book and said, "I never travel without it."

[15] It took a lot of nerve, in 1948, to turn down the first two applications to the course. They were not up to the standard we had set. Jack Brent, who knows the score in a lot of things, reminded me that class members will be judging the course by the kind of people they see in the classroom.

[16] Sir Josiah Stamp, when he was receiving his LL.D. from Western in 1937, underscored the tremendous value of the interpersonal exchanges in a university setting. The peer group, made up of people with varying backgrounds and talents, is a setting for tremendous learning possibilities.

[17] I have learned a lot of things from students. One of the really great contributions came from a student in 'Ad Prac' one day. The case involved was long and not easy to diagnose. This student put his finger on a most important aspect when he burst out, "The trouble with this company is that no one working there is having any fun."

# Establishing the first national school of business

*F.W.P. (Fred) Jones, a successful London businessman and later, Dean of the School (1954-1963), recalls how a group of Canadian businessmen headed by R.G. Ivey, Q.C., a London lawyer and entrepreneur, envisioned establishing Canada's first national school of business administration at Western. Supported by G. Edward Hall, President of the University (1947-1967), they accomplished this task. Dr. Jones describes how this near-miracle came about in this chapter which he wrote in 1978.*

C. B. Johnston (left), Dean of the Business School, 1978-1988, assisted at the ceremonies at which Dr. Jones received an honorary Doctor of Laws degree in 1977. J. Allyn Taylor, Chancellor 1976-1980, is seen congratulating him.

The time was approximately 23.00 hours, the place the University of British Columbia's Faculty Club, the year 1947. At that time, as I remember, the premises were an old army building, well furnished and comfortable, but nothing to compare with the spacious surroundings of today. Dr. George Edward Hall, the newly appointed President of The University of Western Ontario, had just given a very stimulating address to the Vancouver alumni, which I had been invited to attend since, in the pursuit of my activities as Executive Vice-President of a large manufacturer and distributor of building products, I was visiting the West Coast at that time. Dr. Ellis Morrow, then head of the Department of Business Administration, UBC, asked James Coyne Taylor, at that time Professor in the Dept. of Business Administration, UBC, and myself to remain after the meeting. We sat sipping a beverage (something not available on the campus of UWO in those years), and Ellis, who had started the Business Department at UWO, remembered well that it was planned to change it quickly to a graduate school. Out of a 'clear blue sky' he said to Jim and myself: "Dr. Hall is a real builder, but he sounds more dedicated to medicine than to business administration. Fred, when you return, why not talk to Walter Thompson (who was then the Acting Head of the Department of Business Administration, a division of the Arts college), and get Dr. Hall interested in the idea of the graduate school?" Shortly afterwards, I contacted Walter, who said he was so close to the situation that he felt it would be better if I took a small group to the campus to see Dr. Hall. Selected for this meeting were two company presidents: Mr. Gordon Silverwood of Silverwood Dairies*, and Mr. Harold Newell of Andrews Wire and Ironworks, Watford, Ontario. Dr. Hall gave us an appointment and, when we entered his office, one could sense immediately

This picture of Fred Jones was taken at the dinner arranged by faculty to mark the occasion of his retirement from the School in 1974.

* now Silverwood Industries

that Western had entered a new era of expansion and change. We gave him our idea for a graduate school of business administration, in which he was somewhat interested, but he really came alive when we mentioned that we thought Canadian business might pay most of the cost! One could almost sense the sparks in Dr. Hall's mind, as he called for tea and cookies to be served. He was a man who grasped an idea or situation immediately. We left with a definite feeling that, at long last, Canada would have its first graduate school of business administration.

Dr. Hall went to work at once, and I dropped somewhat on the sidelines, as I was very busy with my own business activities. In a very short time, 'G.E.H.' organized a conference of Canadian businessmen to discuss and approve the idea of having Canada's first national school of business administration offering degrees in undergraduate business, M.B.A., executive training courses, doing research, and possibly eventually having a Ph.D Program. They went for it 100%, because by that time he had such 'heavies' as Hugh MacKenzie, President of Labatt's; N. R. 'Buck' Crump, Chairman of CP Railroad; J. R. White, President of Imperial Oil; A. J. Little, Senior Partner Clarkson Gordon; Robert Reid, President of London Life Insurance Company, as well as many other important executives, who agreed to head up a committee to sell the idea to Canadian business. Very quickly, formal plans got under way and a significant conference was called by this group to meet at Western, and the decision was taken. An important immediate request was that Western start a course at once for senior business executives. This was to be modelled along the lines of Harvard's Advanced Management Program. Lloyd Sipherd, as a former professor, attended this conference on behalf of our (Hobbs Glass) company, and stated that the enthusiasm ran very high.

Also, from this conference, a committee was set up to raise money to launch the new School. One of the main purposes of the fund was to buy 'Goodholme' as a base. This spacious house at the north end of Waterloo Street had been built by one of the executives of Supertest Petroleum, and was of such a gigantic size that little work was required to provide adequate classrooms and offices.

### "Lloyd was literally waiting for me at the front door..."

During 1952, my partners and I disposed of our business, and I was casting about for new opportunities. Lloyd Sipherd had already stepped in as Western's first Dean of a school that either had, or was about to have, undergraduate, MBA, and Management Training Course Programs, plus ample funds for research. Learning that I had an offer from the University of Toronto, Lloyd said "As a graduate of Western in business administration, and one who has been close to faculty and students, why don't you come to Western; especially as Toronto still does not have a school, but rather a recently founded Institute of Business Administration?" This appealed to me, because I knew of Western's plans for progress, whereas Toronto was not nearly as far along.

As a consequence, I commenced teaching at Western in January, 1953, and spent an extremely happy year, during which time I was also involved with an 'off campus' Marketing Management Course held in Huntingdon, Quebec. Previous to my arrival on campus, Lloyd Sipherd and Walter Thompson had agreed that, jointly with the Montreal Advertising and Sales Executives Club, the School would sponsor this course.

To my horror, in early January, I learned that introductory work had been done by three other professors, but that from then on I was to

be the entire faculty. To me, this seemed like an unworkable arrangement and placed me in a real quandary. I thought of members of the faculty who might join me. Mr. Jack Wettlaufer seemed like a logical candidate, but he was somewhat reluctant as he had not had very much exposure to the business community at that time. However, from the moment he stood in front of the Marketing Management Course class, he 'stole the show', and from then on, I could have stayed home.

As an illustration of how tight money was in those days, an anecdote might be interesting: in late July, I was informed that my salary was to be increased by $250 – a year. While this does not seem much now, I was very pleased at the recognition...but later I learned that this was to be a raise in name only, since it was to come out of an honorarium I had received for extra time and lectures on the Management Training Course. During the long period in which Lloyd Sipherd and I have been the best of friends, this led to the only real disagreement we ever had. I appreciate now that there was very little that Lloyd could do. Nevertheless, I went for holidays with the pleasant thought that at least I had survived my first semester.

On my return, Lloyd was literally waiting for me at the front door, wanting to see me most urgently. It was to give me the important news that he intended to resign to become a professor (which meant that he would still remain on our faculty), and that he wished to join Dr. Hall in nominating me to become the second dean! This was a complete shock to me, because I realized it would mean almost as heavy a teaching load, plus growing administrative duties. This, of course, was not my aim in leaving the business world. I asked for a period of time to consider this, but agreed to meet with Dr. Hall to learn of some of the things he had in mind. One that came through loud and clear was, if I did not take the job, another appointment would be made which not only might be distasteful to all of the faculty, but

The front door and entrance hall to Goodholme was of 'baronial' proportions and the office the dean occupied was the large library of the former owner of the estate. Writes Dean Jones, "With the office I acquired a mystery, and the rumor still persists that there was a secret compartment behind a panel. But we never found it."

of the simplicity of the job is that for three years the dean could carry out the established custom of entertaining the entire graduating class for dinner in his living room.

How things would change.

---

### *"I was to feel the enormous power and talents of the president."*

---

My first two weeks were extremely pleasant. One of the 'perks' was the extremely baronial office I inherited. This had been the former library of the owner, and I had not been used to such luxury. With the office, I acquired a mystery, and the rumor still persists that there was a secret compartment behind a panel where on several occasions he had exhibited to local friends quantities of antique jewellery. Many of us looked for the hiding place, but never found it.

Another 'weighty' issue I tackled while 'finding my feet' was that my predecessor had never been allowed to have a fire in the office fireplace. This was quickly straightened out over a cup of coffee with the superintendent of Grounds and Buildings, but I was limited to two fires per month, to be confined to special occasions. I mention this to show how small the University was, and the School of Business Administration was even tinier.

Shortly, I was to feel the enormous power and administrative talents of the president. One day I received a telephone call asking me to come over that afternoon. When I arrived, I found Dr. Hall was really laying out for me a plan by which the School was to operate. He had two immediate goals for me, the first a very pleasant one, it was to assist him in raising money to bring the School onto campus. Other items were so distasteful that without further ado we had a prompt 'eyeball-to-eyeball' showdown. For people reading this, there is

also certainly to me. I admit this is an odd way to make up one's mind, but I agreed to give it a try. In 1980, it is interesting to realize how different the process of choosing a dean is: nowadays, it is a 'finely-tuned' committee operation who, over a period of months, give the matter deep consideration. This usually involves students, administration and faculty. Looking back at how we did it then, I think I was most fortunate in being accepted by the faculty, despite the fact that a good percentage felt that this had been pre-arranged. This, of course, was not true, and I stress again that the extra load was accepted reluctantly.

---

### *"When I consider the complexity of the dean's office today, I realize how fortunate I was."*

---

On July 1, 1954, I took over, and when I consider the complexity of the dean's office today, I realize how fortunate I was; the task was so simple then that one could close the office for two or three weeks, and no one would miss you. This is best illustrated by the fact that I had only a full-time faculty of seven, plus an associate dean, myself, and a number of part-time appointments. Credit should be given to Lloyd and Walter for good selection, for almost without exception, everyone of these people has gone on to become deans, associate deans, or administrative officials. Another illustration possibly a piece of philosophy here: if you take on a new job, it is most necessary that there should be a clear-cut understanding with your superior as to exactly how you want to work. If a policy difference emerges, you might as well solve it then. Personally, I was glad that Dr. Hall and I had this discussion and hammered out a working arrangement. In the heated debate, I gained the utmost respect for George Edward Hall. He listened patiently when I told him that I could not work with my faculty on that basis. He said he thought I was completely wrong, but if I was to be Dean, he would support me as long as I worked within the broad guidelines of UWO policy. From that day on we had an extremely stimulating and pleasant relationship. I found him ready to help at all times, and we remained good friends until his untimely death, even though we had some vigorous arguments.

During the summer that followed, the associate dean and I discussed the forthcoming Management Training Course, and we planned several improvements which we thought gave it new lustre. Humorously, on graduation day, I was quite dashed to hear one extrovert telling his boss in a loud 'whisper', "There is Jim Taylor who teaches bookkeeping and Fred Jones who gave us a course in salesmanship." Nevertheless, as usual under Walter's excellent direction, the Management Training Course did reach new heights in enrollment and interest.

In the summer, we had a heartwarming illustration of how an important segment of the business community was supporting us: a group led by Mr. Bill Hamilton (later to become Postmaster General of Canada) came to us to discuss the future of the Marketing Course sponsored by the Montreal Sales and Advertising Club. They were quite amenable to us moving the course to Western and said they would again co-sponsor with us. On the agenda, however, was an item to ask if any of the professors had ever been paid. We told them it had not been possible. They immediately wrote a cheque, and I think the UWO Business School should acknowledge with gratitude one more piece of help given to us.

Today, the course is well established, but the first two or three years gave us many anxious moments.

---

### "After the president suggested we return the Business School to the campus, I conferred with Mr. Ivey."

---

As a result of the 1948 conference of top executives, a strong Advisory Committee had been created. These men for the most part were extremely interested, gave many helpful suggestions, and at times even helped us with special problems that had to do with University policy. When I became Dean, Mr. R. G. Ivey was the Chairman of the Committee. On the one hand, Mr. Ivey has been described as a very successful corporate lawyer, but on the other he was a born entrepreneur at heart and around the world he had built successful plants manufacturing corrugated products. Dr. Hall had thoroughly sold him on the idea of a UWO school of business administration. Additionally, Lloyd Sipherd and myself had on many occasions conferred with Mr. Ivey on problems of business. As a result, I found it easy and pleasant to work with the chairman.

After the president had suggested that we return the Business School to campus, I conferred with Mr. Ivey, and a Toronto meeting of the Advisory Committee was called to discuss this item. The Advisory Board unanimously endorsed the suggestion, but of course there was not enough money available with which to erect suitable quarters. It was left to the chairman, the president, and myself to come up with a plan. The meeting was long, but on conclusion, Mr. Ivey suggested that we take about a three-mile walk to the Toronto Union Station. Arriving there, we both bought newspapers, took separate seats on the train, but later got together to discuss our assignment. When the time came, I moved to his seat and he asked: "How much do you *really* need, in addition to what you have?" Dr. Hall and I had already discussed this question, because we wanted to make sure that the sum raised would be adequate in case the faculty wanted facilities to which we had not given consideration. I named the figure arrived at by the president and myself. I was somewhat amazed to realize that the chairman had been doing some mental arithmetic and stated the exact reduced amount with which we might do the job. To this I tentatively agreed. At that point, he took an envelope out of his pocket, and with a short stub of a pencil did some figuring. Following that, he said "I think I can manage that", which I took to mean that he would call some companies well known to him and undertake to raise the sum. But the next statement left me in a state of very pleasant shock: "Can you give me a few weeks to get the money to you, as I will have to rearrange some securities?" The rest of the journey found me in a daze, and to this day I am not sure whether I adequately thanked him then. But to his memory, I do so now.

I should say that this was the second of his several gifts, and it enabled the Business School to have very adequate premises. Specifically I refer to a conference that he and Dr. Hall had when the faculty advised that we needed better library facilities in the new building. Immediately, he made a large sum available. My successors, no doubt, will know of other gifts, but the move to the campus certainly got the School off to a good start.

The next step was to impart the news to the faculty, because already the people concerned were suggesting that we get on with the job of planning. We were most anxious that the building should be adapted to the 'case method' of teaching, and thus would require other amenities special to schools of business administration as opposed to, e.g., a medical laboratory, or a science department. Accordingly, at a faculty meeting, a one-man committee was set up, and Professor John Nicholson agreed that we would confer with all members of the faculty to get their ideas, and also discuss their advice with the Superintendent of Grounds and Buildings, Mr. John Shortreed. Rather amusing to me were the hundreds of faculty hours spent on designing classrooms that were to be in the shape of a horseshoe. At least 12 different plans were submitted and a shape finally chosen. At that time, we had the idea that each student should sit on a swivel seat for purposes of arguing case points with people around him. This idea would give us many headaches too numerous to detail here, but, by and large, the classrooms turned out to be such a success that very soon other parts of the University were asking to use them for meetings and special sessions.

While planning seems to be a dull activity, in academic life it is not: each teacher had certain requests, and it was quite a job for the faculty as a whole to agree. Something else that plagued us was that evidently we wanted to break what were established rules, and have private offices for each member of the faculty, from assistant professor upwards, with a private telephone. Our reasoning was that, as a microscope or a language laboratory might be to one faculty, so these things were to our operation. Generally, the University administration were very co-operative, and even though we lost some points, the final plans were locked up by having each faculty member initial them.

The construction costs were in line, and the pace at which the building was finished was swift, to the point that we were able to occupy the premises in the summer of 1957.

---

### "The Placement Program has been a real factor in the alliance with business."

---

It is not for me to take any credit for the inception of this idea, since it goes back into the late 1940s when the School was simply a 'Department of Business Administration'.

A good beginning on the idea was made when the faculty set aside an afternoon, and about a dozen Business School graduates and others came up to chair what were called 'Trading Posts'. These revolved around the idea of having the major areas covered by business so that if a student was interested in entering, for example, the financial world, he could ask questions of these men. In cases where students were wavering, for example, between marketing and production, they could be enlightened in both areas. When I came to the School, I found that Neil Armstrong, Director of Administration, among his other duties, had been given three small cubicles on the second floor for student/company interviews. By 1954, there were at least 50 employers coming to our building, and they had a cramped, but quiet, spot in which to interview candidates. In the new building, this program was expanded, and it is my feeling, backed up by talking to businessmen, that this Placement Program has been a real factor in Western's continued alliance with the business community.

---

### "Once again, Canadian business supported the School generously."

---

When the new building was launched, this meant we had to use our entire Research Fund, plus a gift from Mr. R. G. Ivey. Mr. J. R. White, at that time the President of the Imperial Oil Co., and a friend of the School, agreed to take

**Dr. G. Edward Hall, President of The University of Western Ontario (1947-1967). "He was a man who grasped an idea or situation immediately...we left our meeting with him with a definite feeling that, at long last, Canada would have its first school of business administration."**

over the chairmanship of the Advisory Committee and head the fund-raising campaign. This was to be my first experience with how such an effort is undertaken. Working with Mr. White meant several visits to his offices to prepare brochures, compile mailing lists, and to send out letters. While Walter Thompson and I made some personal visits to corporations, I do not think we will ever know how many calls were made by Mr. White to company presidents. Once again, Canadian business supported the School very generously. I was amazed to see that we got very few refusals.

For example, in Montreal we had a great benefactor who had given generously to the first campaign. When Jack White wrote to him the second time, he stated he was fully committed and had to turn our request down, but about three days later we were thrilled to receive a personal letter from this man, stating that while his foundation had no more funds at that time, he himself was attaching a cheque…and a very generous one it was.

At this time I would like to record our gratitude to J. R. White and his hard-working secretary, to whom I give full credit for amassing for us a Research Fund to enable us to do more cases. This in turn would lead to publishing, launching summer research projects, and sponsoring of at least one member of the faculty, per year, to go to another institution for doctoral research, leading to an advanced degree.

### "There were some things forever under discussion."

No doubt, my predecessors went through the same experience, but I could not help noticing during my term of office that there were some things forever under discussion. Sometimes the problems were solved, but others never came to an end. I took over in the midst of a long argument as to what was a normal course load, plus reasonable office hours for student discussion. Looking back over old correspondence, I am amazed to see that some of our most militant professors thought three full courses was a quite satisfactory load, plus a reasonable number of office hours.

Then there was the question of how much a professor should be allowed to indulge in off-campus consulting. To many, a limitation was an infringement on their academic freedom, but finally the University administration laid down an overall policy as a rough guide.

Another endless discussion involved the kind of grading system the School would embrace. At that time, the University was on an entirely numerical system, but others were used; Harvard, for example, graded from 'distinction' to 'unsatisfactory'. We tried to go from 'A+' to 'F'. A radically different approach was simply 'satisfactory' or 'fail'. Finally, Bert Wood (at that time a junior member of the faculty, who had just completed his M.B.A.) rescued us and agreed to study the matter. He took us to the U.S. system of 4, 3, 2, 1, 0. Even so, there were people who clung to the concept of '3+' and '3–'.

I will not belabor here the endless pressures for specialized courses for trade associations, night classes leading to the degrees of B.A. and M.B.A., or additional seminars for groups of the community. But the above will give future students some idea of the long and often stormy faculty meetings that took place.

Especially when we were at Goodholme, there was a real spirit based on the fact that almost all students knew each other. There was, of course, always a feeling that there was a definite undergraduate group, quite separate from MBA students. Even with the School being small, they had their annual formal parties, and something that still makes me shudder—their graduation banquets which rapidly became 'stags'. They started out mildly enough with buns being thrown about the room, but when sugar cubes were used, the parties had to be relocated to points distant from the City. I always remember one such occasion on the old Hamilton Road where the next morning I apologized to a rather irate lady manager. After a 10-minute 'dressing-down', I do not think I ever felt so humble.

Nevertheless, we seemed to have speakers who could rise above the shambles and get across fine messages.

During orientation, students always played quite a role. Early in the game they realized that bewildered fledglings came from all over the world, so students and faculty put on one-day sessions that were helpful to newcomers. As Dean, I was called upon to present some of the objectives of the School. Once, at HMCS Prevost, on such an occasion, a trestle table collapsed with a crash. My talk ended very abruptly.

Student activities in those days resulted in fun as well as in tension. When the School was still in its early days, it was agreed that the students of the Faculty of Medicine would once a year publish the *Gazette,* and so would the business students. At first, everything was peaceful, but finally – I believe it was by the medical students – the publication was hijacked on the premises of *The London Free Press,* who printed these editions. The publishing authorities were good-natured about this feat, but pointed out it was not to happen again. The following year, the other group (the business students not wishing to be outdone!) got their hands on a heavy army tank in which to pick up the *Gazette* and take it to the University. This meant crossing the bridge. In the midst of a Council of Deans meeting, this news reached us, and we had to take immediate action to prevent the project, as the tank would have collapsed the bridge.

Then the School of Nursing got into the act: they thought it would be nice to host a dance and invite MBA students (who at that time were practically all single). When the ratio of married students among them increased, irate wives discovered that their husbands, who presumably were attending evening discussions, were actually dancing with nurses. I, as Dean, did not have a solution to this, but fortunately the students themselves handled the matter.

> *"Parents' Day was a joint venture of student and faculty initiative."*

At this stage, I would like to mention two activities jointly organized by students and faculty: first, Associate Dean Thompson, assisted by Professor Jack Wettlaufer, organized a Parents' Day for undergraduates, which was a tremendous success, since parents not only heard the case discussion, but also the objectives of the School, and had lunch at Somerville House. Also, the MBA students asked to have their parents meet the faculty on graduation day. The lovely garden next to the library was perfect for these most happy occasions. Secondly: the Business Wives' Club was a success from its inception. In this regard, I would like to pay tribute to my deceased wife, Elsie Anne, for her part in getting together a group and starting activities in 1954. Florence Wettlaufer, Eleanor Graham, and others ably assisted. Before my term of office was up, this had grown into a successful and important activity. In addition to social gatherings, they had presentations on investments, life problems, careers, flower arranging, and interior decorating. The wives furthermore expressed interest in having Jack Wettlaufer lead them in a case discussion. In his usual manner, he made this intensely interesting. Before each woman was a lovely rose, and when Jack entered (appropriately clothed in a cap and gown) he was preceded by an aide-de-camp carrying a candelabra. The case was that of *'Mr. & Mrs. Ron Adams'*, involving how much a company could expect from a husband and how much from his wife. Several very ingenious solutions were presented, but none brought down the house like that of a very young MBA's wife who advanced a rather Freudian solution. They tell me that for the first time in his life Jack was left speechless.

About 1959, the Association of Canadian Schools of Commerce and Business approved a motion emphasizing the need for a Doctoral Program for business administration in Canada. Western was one of three universities asked to take the matter under advisement. As a consequence, Dr. D. S. R. Leighton was invited to serve on a one-man committee to look into all aspects of having the School launch this program. His report was submitted in September, 1959 and reviewed by the faculty. As a result, Dr. Leighton gave the matter further consideration, but at the suggestion of the faculty he was joined by Dr. R. K. Ready. In June, 1960, their report was submitted in revised form, and again discussed by the faculty, and approved, subject to discussion with the University administration.

> *"We can take pride in the fact Western was the first to launch, in Canada, a Doctoral Program in business."*

At this point, a difference of opinion occurred; looking back, it now becomes obvious that we were attempting to create a Doctoral Program on the scale of that being operated by Harvard's Graduate School of Business Administration, whereas this was not at all the thinking of the University administration. Rather, they considered admitting doctoral students and having them work with a senior member of the faculty, similar to the efforts being made in other parts of the University. Trying to resolve this, Dr. Leighton and I visited Dr. Hall, and a spirited discussion was held. As a result, Dr. Leighton submitted to me, as Dean, a memo in November of 1960, in which he attempted to reach some rapport with the philosophy of the University, but still drawing our attention to the need for extra faculty, library facilities, scholarships, etc. He commenced by saying that

we should take the first two doctoral students in the academic year 1961-1962 and that they should be chosen to fit into a field in which we were particularly strong. At about the same time the Council of Graduate Studies approved our program, and – as requested by our faculty – once successful, the candidates would receive a 'Doctor of Philosophy'.

It was obvious to me, however, that there were undercurrents in the faculty, causing some dissension concerning the fact that we had not a program similar to that offered by, for example, Harvard or Stanford. Nevertheless, a search started for suitable doctoral candidates, and my recollection tells me that in September of 1961, Alexander Mikalachki was admitted. It is a pleasure to remember at this time that he was our first successful candidate, who was then hired as faculty and has made a great contribution to the School.

It bothered me, however, that there was still a difference of opinion between the University administration and our faculty; one can gain some idea of how wide the gulf was when one looks back at our planned program, which would cost $50,000 per year and accelerate to over $100,000, while the University administration based their ideas on the assumption that it could be done for practically no additional money or faculty time. We on our part may have been too high in our aspirations, but their position was possibly somewhat unrealistic. In hindsight, I would have done some things differently, but nevertheless we can take some pride in the fact that we were the first to launch in Canada, a successful and continuing Doctoral Program in business administration. With the tremendous assistance of my successor, Jack Wettlaufer, the finances were found and the extra faculty were recruited. Sometimes, in any organization – and universities are no exception – one can 'talk a good idea to death', so while our action may have been too fast, to me it was most important that we were under way.

**Richard G. Ivey, Q.C., LL.D., London lawyer, businessman, and philanthropist at the opening ceremonies of the Richard Ivey School of Business Administration Building in 1957.**

---

### *"As our faculty grew, we also were able to recruit some of our own MBA students."*

---

By 1955, it was obvious to me that there was increasing enrollment ahead, whereas our faculty had been shrunk by the illness of one member, in addition to which the 'one and only' Dr. E. J. Fox was forced to resign and leave Canada due to his wife's illness. Ed Fox was one of the great strengths behind the early years of the School. I never saw a man who so completely believed in the work he was doing, and when he stepped onto a platform to discuss a case, his enthusiasm made others 'catch fire'.

Furthermore, some of the junior members of the faculty were delighted to hear of the support which the Advisory Board and Board of Governors were giving to enable them to take doctoral degrees, which in most cases meant a two-year leave of absence.

Knowing the kindness of Harvard's Business School to us in the past, I planned trips there, and was delighted when two young Canadians, D. S. R. Leighton and D. H. Thain, agreed to accept an appointment with us. These visits also gave me the opportunity to get to know, for the first time, two of our faculty members who were on leave and who were undecided about returning to UWO, both of them being U. S. citizens. At this point I might mention that the Canadian border was a great obstacle to attracting a good American-born

teacher and his family; where the man was willing to take the chance, often the wife was fearful of the 'wild and woolly' environment she had heard about. In subsequent recruiting, while we did not turn our back on the U.S.A., we found that in most cases, in those days, it was a useless attempt. That was not particularly important to us, as there was a good pool of available Canadians taking advanced degrees at Harvard. Yet it was somewhat disappointing to lose out on Dr. John McArthur who decided to make a career south of the border – particularly, as by 1980, he had done so well as to be appointed Dean of the Harvard Business School, plus holding several other prestigious appointments.

An amusing sidelight of Harvard recruiting was something about which I still take some teasing from certain 'victims'. When talking to a candidate about coming to Canada, the deal was usually cemented at a famous restaurant in downtown Boston. I found this particularly appealing to husbands and wives, as they were often on an extremely 'hamburger' budget. So, in an intangible way, UWO might be said to owe a debt to the cuisine at the world famous restaurant, Locke Ober.

As our faculty grew, we also were able to recruit some of our own MBA students who would come in on a one or two year appointment, doing teaching and case writing. C. B. Johnston, now Dean; John Graham, the Assistant Dean; Andrew Grindlay, a senior professor; and Bert Wood, a senior professor, are good examples. Three of them came from one class, and the fourth from the following year.

By the time we occupied the new School, or shortly thereafter, we were not only able to meet increased enrollment, but also to provide several sections of Introductory Business, a course open to practically all parts of the University.

Moreover, this gave us a 'breather' whereby we could plan some student activities

**The Richard Ivey School of Business Administration Building on Western's campus.**

and affairs for the business community. As examples, in the autumn of 1953, and again in 1954, we had a 'Business Outlook' seminar. This took the form of an afternoon session and was principally attended by London executives, although it was encouraging to see a number from Toronto, Hamilton and other points in Western Ontario. The formula was to have one from the top ranks of Canadian business, and another from a U.S. academic institution. It might be interesting to note that at the second seminar, we had Professor Paul McCracken, who was then a professor of Business Conditions, based in Ann Arbor, Michigan, and a member of the faculty of the University of Michigan. I mention this because later he held several very important posts in Washington, D.C., and worked very closely with two former U.S. presidents.

On the part of the faculty, there was a feeling that this was not a very large effort, and,

as a consequence, the idea was born to hold a spring seminar. I believe the first one took place in May, 1956. On one of my visits to Harvard, I asked Professor R. K. Ready if he would take charge of the first one, because while in Cambridge, he could get the benefit of Harvard experience on this type of offering. The first seminar was an instant success, and it is a pleasure to see that, as of 1989, the seminar is still held. From the beginning, our own alumni carried a great deal of the planning and teamed up well with at least two or three members of our own faculty. To me, this was a worthwhile effort, since there is a constant danger in schools of business administration of not meeting with the business community often enough.

Over the years, we have had some very dynamic leaders at these seminars, and a good percentage of the participants have been

alumni who now occupy top positions in the world of business and government.

---

*"The period had been pleasant and stimulating even though, at times somewhat frightening."*

---

About 1962, there were a number of thoughts going through my mind which added up to the fact that I should resign as Dean and turn to other things. The period had been pleasant and stimulating, even though at times somewhat frightening, but I felt it was time to transplant myself. Accordingly, I acquainted Dr. Hall with my views and told him that my recommendation for a successor would be Jack Wettlaufer. Jack took office on July 1, 1963, where he proved brilliant as Dean, and I salute him for his great achievements.

## FREDERICK JONES

Frederick W. P. Jones, who was Dean of Western's Business School from 1954 to 1963, was conferred with an honorary Doctor of Laws degree at Western's 224th Convocation in 1977. The following is the citation:

*No one can claim to be a truer son of Western University than Fred Jones. Not only did he graduate from this institution in Honors Business Administration, but also during his academic career he served three tours of duty; first as a Research Assistant and Instructor through the ranks to becoming a Professor and emerging in 1954 as Dean of the Business School.*

*Fred has always shown leadership with a certain panache...in his student days, during the dark days of the depression, he drove one of the very, very few cars on campus and that one boasted a rumble seat! He needed it for even in those days he was going places. As a student he was a member of the Student Council, President of the Debating Society, Business Manager of* The Gazette, *and co-author of a report leading to the establishment of* The Business Quarterly *magazine. He was chosen for the Honor Society, but the appointment that best heralded his consuming interest was Minister of Finance on a University Student Commission. He longed for the financial world but there wasn't a demand for finance whiz-kids in the 'dirty thirties' of his graduation. The awesome fact was there wasn't a demand for any kind of graduate and Fred went into marketing – which translates into selling corn flakes for the Kellogg Company. History records that even when there wasn't much on the tables of southwestern Ontario in those desperate days corn flakes sales were on the rise. Thus was launched his business career which led to operating his own business in Nova Scotia to returning to London where he served his company in the glass industry in several capacities, ending as President of his company.*

*It was then that he returned to academic life. By his own admission he claims not to be an academic but confesses to a great love of teaching. His teaching style is to tell students how it is done in the business world with a dash of how it ought to be done. Evidence of his skill is found in the fact that his Investment Management course was the most popular ever taught for he knew whereof he talked.*

*Ever since graduation Fred had an active interest which he shared with others – that of seeing a Business School formed on Western's campus. Finally in 1947 as a self-appointed Chairman, along with two other business graduates, he approached the President with the idea which was quickly acted upon. His fulfilled dream now houses the leading Business School in Canada.*

*In that same year he helped with the first large fund-raising drive from which emerged Thames Hall. It is surely a mark of his devotion to the University that he has served on every fund-raising drive during the past 30 years.*

*Fred participated in the organization and faculty of the first Management Training and Marketing Courses. He helped organize a Grants-In-Aid Program at the School and was one of the driving forces in the conception of Canada's first Doctoral Program in Business Administration.*

*Early in his career he foresaw the necessary interface of business and government. During the war he was director of a division of Wartime Prices and Trade Board. He has served as Chairman of an Ontario Commission Researching the Marketing of Agricultural Products; supervised an OEC study on the future of the Thunder Bay area; organized and was Chairman of the Province of Ontario subsidized ARF and acted on the Central Board.*

*Fred Jones' name is to be found as a director of an illustrious number of companies in the fields of finance, manufacturing and service.*

*Mr. Chancellor, in the name of the Senate, I ask you to confer the Degree of Doctor of Laws, honoris causa, on Frederick William Price Jones, an outstanding business and academic leader who has maintained his ties and devotion to this University in a way which is unique. He is himself a unique man whose reputation as a fly-fisherman is only matched by his ability as a gardener to get the maximum capital gain from a package of lettuce seeds!*

## RICHARD GREEN IVEY, Q.C., LL.D.

Richard G. Ivey, a London lawyer, businessman and philanthropist, died in 1974. It is his name that is on the Business School for in 1948 he became the first Chairman of the Advisory Committee for the School and he led the fund drive which made possible the building of the School. His interests extended well beyond the bricks and mortar however and he also financed the first Canadian MBA Program, the first Management Training Course as well as the first Ph.D Program in Business. He also donated to the School's Research Fund as well as to the continuing Plan for Excellence which placed Western's Business School in a leadership position in Canada during his lifetime.

Both his son, Richard M. Ivey (who later became Chancellor of Western), and his grandchildren, Richard W. and Rosamond (Ivey) Thom are graduates of the School.

Mr. Ivey remained Chairman of the Advisory Committee until he was elected Chancellor of the University in 1955, a position he held until 1961.

In 1954, the University granted him an honorary Doctor of Laws degree in recognition of his contribution. The following is the citation written and delivered by Dr. G. Edward Hall, President of the University at that time, at the Convocation ceremonies.

*On a summer's Saturday afternoon one will see a tractor pulling multiple mowers cutting grass on a beautiful rolling property north of London. The operator will be Richard Ivey, a director of Canadian International Paper Company and The Bank of Montreal. And on weekday evenings from spring to fall you will find him in his greenhouses or gardens, if you*

*can find him at all. As President of Northern Life Assurance Company of Canada, as a director of Bathurst Power and Paper Company, The Royal Trust Company, Container Corporation of America, John Labatt Limited, Canadian General Insurance Company, and as the Senior partner in the law firm established by his father, it is no wonder that many winter evenings are spent as a dispatcher operating his miniature passenger and freight trains through model tunnels, past realistic stations and over diminutive bridges. But this is not the reason why he became President of the London Street Railway.*

*Mr. Ivey is a stirring example of the successful businessman who has learned how to relax and how to live and how to enjoy those things in life which are fundamental and real. And it was he, this internationally known, busy Londoner, who still had time to give to the University.*

*When the School of Business Administration was established five years ago, an Advisory Committee to the School was created with members from the Board of Governors, this University staff and from among Canadian business leaders. Mr. Ivey has been Chairman of that Committee since its inception. We all realize that the success of any committee is indubitably associated with the calibre of the chairman. The success of the School of Business Administration is a reflection of the success of the Committee under the chairmanship of this distinguished barrister and businessman whom we honor today.*

*Mr. Chancellor, it is a pleasure indeed to request you, on behalf of the Senate of the University, to admit to the degree of Doctor of Laws, honoris causa, Richard Green Ivey, who in indicating his willingness to accept this honor stated, "Anything I may have contributed to the School of Business Administration of The University of Western Ontario was gladly given and with a desire of participating in a most important and worthwhile educational project."*

# The alligator years

*For 40 years, Jack Wettlaufer played a leading role in shaping and developing the Western Business School. In fact, for thousands of people, Jack Wettlaufer and the Western Business School are synonymous. Both emerged as leaders, and outstanding contributors to management development for Canadian business.*

*In 1988, Jack recalled his 'alligator years' as Dean from 1968 to 1978.*

Just as one likes to be able to say that one's world is unfolding as it should, I would like to be able to write that the current admirable state of the School of Business Administration at The University of Western Ontario was already clear to me that afternoon, now more than 30 years ago, when Dr. G. Edward Hall, then President of the University, called me into his office and told me I was going to be made Dean of the School of Business Administration. Unfortunately, I can't write that, because at the time the only emotion I experienced was abject terror. And it was terror that saved me. When you're up to your neck in alligators, the last thing you're calm enough to think about is crawling out of the swamp.

The tiny institution I took over that afternoon in 1963, however, has nevertheless become the preeminent business school in Canada, and one of the leading business education centres of the world – an institution, as President Sherwood Fox described it, offering "a type of academic training for business which would in name and principle be unique in Canada." I can rightfully take, perhaps, a fraction of the credit. More than most other schools, the development of the School at Western has been a team effort. Needless to say, the School has grown and evolved as business and capitalism have matured. Thanks, however, to my invaluable colleagues who worked together to consolidate our gains in the 1960s and early 1970s and beyond. I can honestly say that Western has been much more than a spectator to the process of its own growth. We have all been a lively participant.

But I knew none of that when I arrived at the Faculty of Business in 1948 via Waterloo College. My route to Western, like many of the School's business alumni, followed service in Europe during the Second World War. The influence of the war is, I suspect, responsible for much of the energy that has characterized North American business in the past 40 years. Having emerged from an undergraduate

Business Administration Course held jointly by Western and Waterloo in 1950, I found myself the following year in the second Master of Business Administration class in Western's history. I planned to teach in industry, and had already begun negotiations with the General Motors Institute in Flint, Michigan, when Walter Thompson, then Assistant Dean, asked me if I wanted to join the new Business faculty.

The course was Business 30. This meant I would teach 35 women in the Secretarial Science Department. Classes took place in one of two classrooms in the basement of University College. My salary was $3,800, which was more than the $2,400 a year Professor Lloyd Sipherd earned in the early 1930s, but much less than I would need to establish my fortune. The department was small but busy. In 1952, I was also appointed Acting Alumni Director of the University. It was the first of many personnel shortages I was to experience in the next 30 years.

The very smallness and seeming insignificance of the School in those early days is testimony, I think, to the difficulties that surround the planning of any educational institution – particularly if it is to be one of any significance in the future. Oh yes, we were converts down in the basement of University College: our difficulty lay not in believing in the future of the Business School, but in convincing others.

The notion of an independent business school had come from the business sector – a source of intelligence and feedback to which the School has remained closely tied ever since. These links we maintain to the 'real' world are one reason my eloquent colleague, Walter Thompson, deemed us 'the businessman's business school.' Dr. Hall had convened a meeting of Canadian business leaders, in 1948, to ask what the Business School could do for the business community: the MBA Program and our Management Training Courses were the direct result. The

Discussing the long range plans for the School were (left to right) Dr. G. Edward Hall, Col. D.B. Weldon, Jack Wettlaufer, R.G. Ivey and Harold Rae then President of Canadian Oil and Chairman of the School's Advisory Committee (1961-1967).

School has turned to the business community as one source of suggestions and ideas ever since.

While the School was beginning to train its own faculty, we still relied heavily on Harvard for academic staff, a practice that continued well into my tenure as Dean. Before we could grow our own faculty, I was to travel North America to inspect other programs and to recruit the expertise we needed to become a world-class business school. I traveled to fascinating if unexpected places, as befitted the catch-as-catch can atmosphere of those early days. One afternoon I was rummaging through alumni lists when Dr. Hall, then President of

the University, called to ask if I'd like to go to California. Dr. Hall had a habit of kidding me, and I was certain he was joking. "Sure," I said. "Anytime. When do I leave?"

"Ten o'clock tomorrow morning," he said. That was the beginning of Western's long-standing relationship with the Stanford Research Institute, which was developing a far-reaching economic study that would later lead to a national crisis in Parliament and the first invocation of closure to end the infamous pipeline debate. I noticed then, for the first but not last time, how hard Americans worked – a habit among our Harvard colleagues that impresses me to this day. If we have done well at Western, and produced a breed of manager and management of renown, it is in large part due to the dedication to professionalism and hard work that has been a staple of our curriculum since day one. One need only ask our alumni for proof of this fact. They still have their Honors Business Administration (HBA) and Master of Business Administration (MBA) scars, and they're proud of them.

Those who attended our first and subsequent Management Training Courses were hard-working too – to say nothing of hard-playing! I'm surprised I survived those 'workfests'. The second course – an intensive workshop in marketing management – was the brainchild of the Montreal Advertising and Sales Club, which had approached McGill University unsuccessfully before approaching Western. Fred Jones, who was then a professor at the School, and I traveled by train to Huntingdon, Quebec to give a series of weekend seminars with roughly 40 marketing executives. Once the course was successfully completed, we informed the Montreal Advertising and Sales Club that we would run the course on the conditions it be operated in London and was open to applicants from across the country. That was the birth of the Marketing Management Course – the first of its kind in North America. To this day, it and all the School's short-term Management Courses, are dynamic lessons in what happens when people gather in an environment where teaching and learning are indistinguishable. Every five years those who have taken the Management Training Course have reunions which are educational in a different way.

## THE EARLY '40s AND '50s

What I remember as noteworthy about the late 1940s and early 1950s, among much else, is the kind of graduates we were attracting. Half of each class comprised veterans from the war, while the other half consisted of youngsters fresh out of high school or Undergraduate Programs. The difference in age was substantial. In those veterans, however, lay much of the energy that has characterized international capitalism since the Second World War – a period of unprecedented growth and expansion. Forced to theorize about it today, I would say most of those veterans felt they had leased part of their life to the defence of a political and economic system they were now eager to be a part of and prove workable. The irony of these developments for me, myself a veteran, was that my father always wanted me to become a businessman. "You could be a lot wealthier," he often insisted. Wealthier, yes, but more involved, at a more seminal level, in the business of business? More involved in North American corporate culture, which I am certain will eventually emerge as the most vigorously successful accomplishment and activity of the twentieth century? I doubt it.

Then as now, we on faculty worked hard. Shortly after I was made an Assistant Professor, I began teaching several sections of a course entitled Business 20 (classes were comprised of 125 students a section), plus my regular teaching load. My specialties became Personnel, Industrial Relations and Administrative Practices, Walter Thompson having introduced the latter at Western for the first time anywhere in Canada. The results of all this teaching (and learning, I might add – the courses I taught were as instructive to me as to my students!) were tangible if nowhere near as bountiful as they are today. In 1963 we graduated 63 M.B.A.s and 66 B.A.s.

"Those who attended our first and subsequent Management Training Courses were hard-working – to say nothing of hard-playing! I'm surprised I survived those 'workfests'."

**"a title makes an enormous difference...in the form of more work."**

I had been serving as Associate Dean and later as Acting Dean when Fred Jones became ill. On the fateful day Dr. Hall called me into his office and instructed me to fill Fred's enormous shoes, I was treated to a shocking realization: a title makes an enormous difference, mainly in the form of more work. I thought I understood the administration of a school of business that stood free from the rest of the University, but a week on the job, in 1963, convinced me I had merely been paddling to keep the ship afloat. Suddenly, in addition to my other responsibilities, I was in charge of admissions, hiring, faculty appointments, and the general management of relationships and programs that make up any school in any university. That year I began regularly to thank God for the presence of Florence, my wife, and Jean Strangways, my secretary for 18 years.

In hindsight I realize that the School I inherited was about to embark on a period of growth that was to transform it from a sturdy young business school into a mature institution. There was a lot of work to be done. For instance, there was no Faculty Appointments Committee – Dr. Hall had been handling that. I was a little concerned about my own appointment, if truth be told, because I had ascended to the exalted ranks of full professorship from associate only a week before Dr. Hall appointed me Associate Dean. What, I inquired of him, was the senior faculty going to think?

My management style was very different from Dr. Hall's. Dr. Hall ran The University of Western Ontario in all its parts as a strict, but fair, patrician. He never let much slip from his sight. Despite the dissent that raged at Western during the 1960s – and, I might add, at every

North American university worth its salt – and despite later criticism of the president's autocratic ways that perhaps inevitably fell upon his shoulders in turbulent times, he was an extraordinary administrator. His genius lay in knowing that a relatively young university such as Western could not be good at everything instantly.

He knew the young Western had to choose an intellectual specialty, conquer it, and become outstanding in that subject before broadening its hopes and horizons. When he created a business school separate and independent of Western's other faculties, he did so in the conviction that the School of Business Administration should rise to become the best business school in Canada. It would thereby enhance the reputation of the rest of the University. Needless to say, Dr. Hall was a man whose vision and standards were extremely exacting – which is why, for instance, I, 'Jacques' Wettlaufer, found myself, in my second year as Dean, in Quebec at Trois Pistoles Summer School learning French. We were, I believe, the first business school in the country to try to make bilingualism and biculturalism a fact of business life. Francophone students from Quebec have made an important contribution to the School.

**"somehow, the future came together."**

I was faced with more prosaic problems, however. Three in particular would shape the years ahead: money and lack of it, the need to do more research that would firmly establish our Doctoral Program, and the need to develop Canadian 'cases', or company-related business

problems, for use in our classrooms. At least, I like to think now that I had it all organized that way in my head back then. In fact, I just put out one fire after another. Somehow, with the tireless help of my colleagues, the faculty of the School, our students, and about three miracles a week, the future came together.

My first problem was with the Ford Foundation. We needed some $315,000 to help fund our Doctoral Program, which at that point was in disarray and in need of leadership. But that year the Ford Foundation reversed their policy of funding business-related interests. So, Dr. Hall and I journeyed to New York and convinced the Foundation to extend their help to us – in other words, to reverse their reverse. I felt like Oliver Twist begging for more. To my amazement, we were successful in our quest. It certainly felt great to win one right off the bat.

But money was only one of our needs. My colleagues and I made lists of areas we felt needed work in the School. There were two consistent complaints: faculty and curriculum development, and the virtual absence of both. The faculty lacked confidence. We knew we were a good school, but we enjoyed no international reputation and no international recognition. Recognition does majestic things to the soul of a professor. By 1964 we had made progress in this regard, however, thanks to David Leighton, a graduate of the Harvard Business School who had joined our faculty. With David's help we organized the National Conference on International Business, whose keynote speaker was Mitchell Sharp, the Canadian politician. Coupled with our rejuvenated Ford Foundation program, the resulting international faculty exchanges were great confidence builders for all our faculty. Many of us, after all, had been home-grown at Western. Visiting professors from Columbia, Michigan State, Harvard, New York University, UCLA, and Cornell, visited, lectured and held conferences during their visits to Western. Our faculty pumped them for solutions to universal faculty problems. Quite apart from the new ideas these visitors injected into our midst, they also served to prove to both our students and our faculty what I had suspected all along: our people were just as good as any at other institutions. By 1966, the visits had blossomed into an International Management Course, the first of its kind in the world and the third such program at Western. And it was still only 1965!

All this was going on at once, and made for overworked professors. The mulish workload on our faculty had been recognized as a problem at least since 1963, when the Long Range Planning Committee – headed by Professors Andrew A. Grindlay, R.K. Ready and Donald H. Thain – pointed out that too few teachers were taking on too many tasks.

---

### "We've got a school that is going to be world famous ..."

---

Roughly thereabouts, I was chosen one of Western's delegates to the international meeting of Commonwealth universities at The University of London. The other London, that is. My dean's shoes were still so new they squeaked. Still, there I was, in attendance at garden parties and dinners hosted by Her Majesty Queen Elizabeth and the Lord Mayor of London. I found myself in the august but reassuring company of Dr. Hall, Col. D.B. Weldon, Chairman of Western's Board of Governors, and Dr. Mark Inman, who at the time was Vice-President, Academic Planning at Western. At one point during lunch the late Dr. John Deutsch, Principal of Queen's University and I were invited to lunch at the London School of Economics with Sir Arnold Plant and Sir Sidney Hawke, who ran the famous London School of Economics. We were halfway through the cold entrée when Sir Arnold turned to me

and said, "Oh, yes, and who on your faculty is world famous?"

Instantly, the Stratford, Ontario boy in me popped out. "Actually, we don't have anyone who is world famous," I replied. "We've got a school that is *going* to be world famous."

Sir Sidney had a laugh at that – as well the Director of the London School of Economics might. Traditional business schools were, and still are, run on a 'star' system: a professor shines as an individual, and so reflects light indirectly upon the school where he teaches. Not so at the School of Business Administration at The University of Western Ontario, as I hastened – most respectfully, of course, to point out to his Lordship. At Western, the School and the team that comprises it – faculty and students alike – are the one and only important body. Individuals work to make the School outstanding before they administer to their own careers. This isn't to say we have no internationally recognized scholars of business here at Western, because we do. I am convinced, however, that Western's is the only way a business school can operate – particularly when it is a school such as ours, which has always prided itself on providing what business needs. If there is a Western brand of management in the international business community today, it is a style characterized by dependable teamwork. I do not claim it does not have its downside risks. Our philosophy can make professors less marketable to other neighborhoods of the academic community than they might be if their individual stars were encouraged to shine ever more brightly than the others around them, or at least according to the wattage of their reputations. It is for that very reason that our professors take a substantial risk when they

join Western, and it is why we are very, very careful when we select them. But I remain convinced, having spent a lifetime studying organizational behavior, that Western's approach to academic life is the only viable one if teaching is to be one's first concern. I am convinced as well that Western's brand of management is the way of the future, when international economic and financial co-operation will be ever more important. And if what I saw on a trip to Japan in 1980 is any indication, the best Japanese managers agree with me. I think of an administrator, be it in a classroom or on the shop floor, as being a servant as well as a leader. I believe business must serve people, and to lead them by the example of that service. There are many people who are uncomfortable with the notion. Dr. Hall was one of them. But times change, and I think the times want and will continue to want the species of manager Western's School of Business takes pride in producing.

It was during this time, in the mid-1960s, that I also met Sir Philip Sherlock, Vice-Chancellor of the University of the West Indies. He asked me to lecture to his colleagues in Jamaica, Barbados and Trinidad about business education. I did, and the result was our joint program with the University of the West Indies. Within two years, thanks largely to the efforts of Walter Thompson, we had earned a formal contract to provide advice and counsel to the University of the West Indies via the federally-funded Canadian International Development Agency (CIDA). We helped Dr. Marshall Hall of Jamaica and Dr. Eric St. Cyr of Trinidad develop business programs and indigenous case materials. Time and time again, Western employed suggestions from the larger business community to improve its syllabus. This willingness, this open-mindedness, is responsible for a good deal of our success.

Studied rationally, there is absolutely no reason why the top business school in Canada should be found in London, Ontario. But in London we are, for reasons that in hindsight are clear. McGill and The University of Toronto defaulted on the opportunity to develop top business schools: in most universities until quite recently, business was a vulgar, almost profane word, much the way journalism has been more recently and medicine was decades ago. But Western couldn't afford to be snobbish intellectually. London, Ontario also possessed a surprisingly high concentration of business talent, which was very supportive. The ethic of capitalism flourished in London, while the principle of service to the outside community flourished here at the University.

Needless to say, we've had our share of successes. The list of senior Canadian executives who graduated from Western is far too long to reproduce here, even though many are household names.

But our success preyed upon us too. By 1966, a Long Range Planning Committee had produced a hard-hitting report that insisted the School grow bigger. We immediately planned a new addition to our building, with what I am proud to say was great foresight, thanks in large part to the efforts of faculty such as John Nicholson, Mike Leenders and Neil Armstrong. Traditionally, schools are designed to work conceptually like a triangle, with a dean at the top and a lot of undergraduates along the base. You make money off the undergraduates, spend it on the MBAs and derive your prestige from doctoral students. In a traditional university setting, the best professors tend to teach the doctoral students, and pay less attention to those down the intellectual ladder.

We weren't having any of that. Our tradition, having grown out of Harvard's model and our close association with the business community, had made us a graduate school of practical business training from the start. Our

task was not easy. How could we develop visibility and a reputation for a new M.B.A. degree and still maintain an outstanding Undergraduate Program? Our answer was to enroll 500 MBAs and only 300 undergraduates, in the hope we would be seen as an MBA school. This is not to imply that the HBA Program is not an integral part of our School and its philosophy, for it is. Publicly, however, we needed to position ourselves as a specialist school. To this day, there are three applicants for every place we have in the HBA and MBA Programs.

At the same time, instead of erecting a magnificent edifice and then trying to fit into it, we designed the present Business School headquarters to do exactly what we wanted it to do – which was to allow faculty a maximum of time for research and teaching: to provide semi-circular classrooms with swivel seats for the greatest interaction and participation; to allow the installation of audio visual and computer capabilities.

As I traveled from campus to campus across North America, I watched for new ideas. And I saw how new and original – intentionally or otherwise – many of our School's techniques were. We have never been stuffy. When we want to talk to the bright lights – or at least to the bright lights at other institutions – we invite them in. Our traditional academic strengths – management and decision-making techniques – are exercised constantly, thanks to the intellectual contributions of visiting Ford scholars and our home-grown faculty. Jack McDougall, for

instance, pioneered Western's research on the responsibilities of directors, the first (but certainly not the last) study of its kind in Canada.

---

*"Our commitment to excellence has become one of the ideals of this School and all who pass through it."*

---

## THE TURBULENT 1960s

Our goals did not change as the turbulent 1960s progressed; they widened. If there was one commodity we all sought, it was excellence in everything we did, from the quality of instruction to the state of our facilities to the degree of professionalism we tried to impart to our students – even to the point of encouraging what was for a long time a student-originated dress-code. We realized, too, that the educational requirements of the country were expanding rapidly. By the mid-1960s we planned to double the number of students enrolled at the School. Finally, we recognized that while McGill and Toronto had ignored business as a field of intellectual and pedagogical concern in the early 1950s, they had since begun to upgrade their business schools, and had created their own MBA Programs. So there was competition with which to contend. Needless to say, we had no intention of relinquishing our reputation as the best business school in Canada and one of the outstanding schools in the world. But to maintain it we had to encourage faculty research, all the while not compromising the quality of our teaching at either the undergraduate or the graduate level. The Western-Harvard link, strong to this day, was helpful to that end, particularly on matters of recruiting. Harvard's example reminded me constantly that a dean ought never to hire someone who is merely good; he must hire only truly excellent teachers. In the years that ensued, our faculty often taught shorthanded amid a multitude of student complaints until we found the right, the 'excellent' person for the job. On that count we never compromised. I like to think our commitment to excellence has become one of the ideals of this School and all who pass through it.

Towards the end of the 1960s, Western began to experience the campus strife that had disrupted most North American universities. Dr. Hall, with his authoritarian tendencies, found himself in the middle of it all. At the Business School, the strife was understandably more limited; it actually derived mainly from the faculty, who felt overworked and under-appreciated! Together with the students, the faculty discussed the problems of social and organizational discipline, out of which came several cases and a course on Managing Change, under the leadership of David Kuechle – a course, I might add, that is immensely popular to this day. Once again the School of Business Administration's outward gaze paid off, focused as it was on the public world, rather than solely upon concerns within the 'ivory tower'.

---

### *"The case method has always encouraged breadth of mind among students."*

---

The case study method, for its part, has always worked admirably at our School, and is, I think, a first-rate expression of the aims of a Business Program that has always encouraged breadth of mind among its students. After all, Western's School of Business Administration was founded by two Classics professors. While administrative studies had always been important, and one of the School's strengths, advances in the behavioral sciences evolved into business-related human relations courses. Computers, on the other hand, placed new emphasis on 'figure studies'. While we consider ourselves 'the businessman's business school,' we also enjoy the flavor of our 'small' school where a liberal education is an essential tool of any thorough-minded capitalist – and I think of a liberal education as the ancient Greeks did, as 'one fit for a free man.' To my mind, capitalism at its best is an opportunity to fit theory to action, to serve freedom and enterprise as inseparable and mutually supporting ideals. To be offered the opportunity to impart these ideals to bright and highly motivated students is, to my mind, one of the most exciting ways I can imagine to have spent as life's work. Certainly that belief lay behind my decision to turn down the presidency of a university on more than one occasion. I was more interested in excellence than I was in prestige. It all depends what one wants to do with one's life.

I think the National Centre for Management Research and Development, the School's current project, is a step towards the realization of those ideals.

To me the spirit of the School has always been important. The first year of the HBA and MBA Programs have always been the 'killers', but the ordeal is what binds a class together for years after it leaves the School. Today's Business Programs are more integrated and offer students a broader course selection than they could in the 1960s – a reflection of how much more sophisticated business practices have become. Beneath the new methods, however, lies one sustaining belief of the faculty here at Western – that business is first and last a 'judgment art', as Walter Thompson once so well described it, one whose basic principles are nailed to the firm ground of common sense and courage.

I think too that the feeling of community among students in the Business School is one reason so many of them wish they could return to London, Ontario to live. Am I exaggerating this desire? Perhaps, but many do return.

And it wasn't always easy to live in London, especially as summer Management Programs got underway. Soon enough we had to ask ourselves whether we ought to investigate the expansion of Spencer Hall, which at the time was a residence for women. I had visited Neil Armstrong, our extremely capable former Director of Administration, out at the Banff School of Fine Arts, where he had gone as Administrator. He was having difficulties filling rooms. As a result of witnessing this, Associate Dean Bud Johnston and I decided we didn't want to be in the bedroom business. Then luck struck. We had a call from Cedric Ritchie, Chairman of the Bank of Nova Scotia. He wanted us to help the bank build and design a training centre. A light bulb clicked as Bud Johnston and I discussed the matter. Why not invite the Bank of Nova Scotia to consider Spencer Hall as a possibility?

We knew we had them sold when Cedric Ritchie and Gordon Bell, the bank's President, walked through Spencer's magnificent front door. "That's the same marble we have at the bank," Cedric said. The result was a joint venture between the University and the Bank of Nova Scotia, known as The Spencer Hall Foundation, which included a dormitory and technologically up-to-date classrooms. I only wish we could offer our HBA and MBA students the same intense educational experience that comes of living and working together. I'm not sure they would agree, however. Enough is enough.

**"The Advisory Committee was manned by individuals who did things their own way."**

I don't think very much would have been possible at the School had it not been for our Business Advisory Committee. Each member of that committee, was a powerhouse in his own right. Each one of them brought his experience and seasoned judgment to bear on virtually every kind of problem that presented itself to the School. One of the first members I met was Harold Rae, then President of Canadian Oil – at least until it was taken over by Shell Oil.

Harold subsequently resigned from Canadian Oil, but was still Chairman of the Advisory Committee at Western. One day he told me the story of being taken over by Shell. I told him I thought it was a fascinating tale – one the class ought to hear. Why didn't he come down? But Harold had a better idea, he often did, which was why, I suppose, Shell liked his company so much. Not only would he come down, he told me, he'd bring Vaisy Ash, the President of Shell who had engineered the takeover. "Fine," I said, wondering what kind of violence we were going to witness on the floor of the classroom.

Several weeks later, Harold, Vaisy and I flew into London from Toronto on Vaisy Ash's private plane. The classroom was jammed.

Harold started the story. He had just arrived home from a game of golf one Saturday and was having a drink with his wife when three Cadillacs – black, black, black – whispered into the driveway. It was Vaisy Ash from Shell, thoughtfully dropping by to tell Harold he was about to have his beloved company bought out from under him. And all because it was such a well-run company. Gentlemen to the end. The class was as instructive for the participants as it was for the students: neither Vaisy nor Harold knew what the other had been doing in the course of the takeover. I only wish we had made a video of the entire discussion. But I am sure it lives on vividly in the mind of everyone in the classroom that afternoon.

**The development of Spencer Hall as a training centre was a joint venture between the University and the Bank of Nova Scotia.**

The Advisory Committee was consistently manned by individuals, entrepreneurs who did things their own way. It was at the height of the campus strife at Western, for instance, when Dr. Hall was roundly reviled as the academic administrative equivalent of Genghis Khan, a cad and a bounder, that the entire Advisory Committee – and I proudly include myself among them – paid public tribute to Dr. Hall for being the strong-minded visionary he was. It stirred me to work with men like that. Together the Advisory Committee's members constituted what was and still is easily the most knowledgeable, most prestigious board of directors in Canada. A list of their names reads like the *Financial Post Directory of Directors.*

Jack Brent, an HBA class of 1931 graduate of the School and Chairman of IBM Canada, was unique! When the 1968-1969 term rolled up, the School of Business Administration was once again – surprise – looking for money. The five-year Ford Foundation grant was coming to an end. While the Ivey Foundation had very generously donated $403,000 to be used for the same purposes as the Ford grant, project and case research had developed insatiable appetites. By 1968-1969 we were consistently returning to the Advisory Committee for scholarship money, all too often on an *ad hoc* basis. One day, the problem was finally too visible to ignore, I swallowed my pride, approached the Advisory Committee and asked for $1,500,000. I like to think of it as the day the rain came in a year of great drought. Jack Brent responded by giving me an office and a secretary at IBM's Toronto headquarters. He also offered me a number of crucial lessons in the mysterious art of corporate fund-raising – lessons he imparted in the course of over 100 calls we made together.

Jack always insisted on several ground rules for these calls. Never talk to anyone but the chief executive officer was one of them. Another was always arrive at an appointment

John E. Brent, who became Chairman of the Board and Director of IBM Canada and also a Director of IBM World Trade Corporation, New York, "is woven into the fabric of Western Business School." He is a graduate (Class of '31), a founding member of the Advisory Committee and, in 1968, became Chairman. In 1972 he received a LL.D. from Western, the citation in part, was as follows: "It was Alfred North Whitehead who said: 'a great society is a society in which men of business think greatly of their functions'. John Brent is such a man."

15 minutes early; that meant you usually got an extra 15 minutes with the chief executive officer in question, especially as the person cooling his brogues in the front office was Jack Brent, Chairman of the Canadian arm of the largest computer company in the world. The third main rule was that we always knew exactly what we wanted and why we wanted to get it. Jack Brent was allergic to fancy brochures. For that reason he relied instead on short introductions, straightforward requests for money, detailed demonstrations of where the money would be spent, plus follow-ups later on of how it was in fact used.

---

*"Jack Brent offered me crucial lessons in the mysterious art of corporate fund-raising."*

---

And these rules were inviolable. I well remember one late night in the Chateau Champlain in Montreal. Jack and I were in town with Captain Joe Jeffery, the Chairman of the Board of Western, and Dr. Carlton Williams, the University's President. Power Corp's Paul Demarais, a member of our Advisory Committee, was kindly hosting a luncheon the next day with the presidents of all our associate companies in Montreal. The evening prior to the luncheon, Jack invited us all to his room. He then proceeded to make each of us recite our upcoming fund-raising pitches. I don't think anyone has ever taken that approach with Joe Jeffery or Carlton Williams before or after. I admit I breathed out a lot. But everybody recited, and willingly, for Jack was a stickler for details and there were to be no exceptions.

It worked. Thanks to Jack Brent and the Advisory Committee, we raised $1,500,000 in two years.

Then there was my visit to Don MacPherson, President of General Motors, with Allan Burton, the Chairman of Simpson's, who succeeded Jack Brent as Chairman of the Advisory Committee in 1976. Allan and I planned to take his Rolls Royce to General Motors' plant in Oshawa. But while we both knew Don MacPherson well, it didn't seem like quite the right car for a woe-is-us fund-raising expedition, especially given the worthy products produced by Mr. MacPherson's company. So we drove down to Oshawa in a GM Pontiac owned by Allan's chauffeur. We arrived on time at the front door of the General Motors' building. The receptionist announced us and we ascended by elevator to the executive offices. Don's secretary greeted us and smiled warmly at Allan Burton. "Dean Wettlaufer," she said, "I've been looking forward to meeting you after all these years." Apparently, with his small round glasses and scholarly appearance, Allan Burton looked more like a dean than I did. The remark must have kept him awake for years. I, by contrast, slept that much more soundly.

The fund-raising responsibilities of a dean, however, never end. We began to look to our alumni as another source of ideas and financial aid. Project Old Boy, the second phase of our 10 year fund-raising effort, was the direct result. Neil Armstrong and I developed a presentation which focused its hypnotic hectoring on Western's alumni. We first presented it to an older group in Toronto. I had very high expectations. I thought they were going to stand up and applaud and cry real tears and say "Neil and Jack boy, go for it, it's wonderful."

Instead, they gave us what I can only characterize as hell. "What right have you got that the only time we've heard from you as alumni is now, when you want money?" they said. "It's about time you did something for us."

I was completely unprepared for such a reaction. Fortunately I don't bruise easily, and it was later, upon reflection, that we saw this as an opportunity to introduce our so-called 'Birthday Parties', or reunions for our alumni. It was 1973. Again, we saw networks as key not only to a strong business school but also to a healthy post-school professional life as well. Initially we thought to devise an advisory committee consisting mainly of company presidents. But Urban Joseph, then a young 'Turk' in Toronto with the Toronto-Dominion Bank, signed up 1,000 members in a Toronto-based alumni club before we knew what had happened. By 1976-1977, we had two more clubs – one in Montreal and another in Calgary. Others were started later in Edmonton and Vancouver. The list of people who breathed life into these alumni programs is too long to recite but they know who they are and I am forever grateful to them.

It was as a result of their efforts during a series of 'Birthday Parties' to commemorate the 50th anniversary of the School in 1973 that my wife Florence witnessed her first alumni ritual at the Calgary Birthday Party when we passed through that city on our way to Vancouver. I stopped to make a speech to a gathering of graduates in Calgary, and we never got any further west! Why? Because every time I opened my mouth to begin the speech, some new and cosmic event would occur, be it the sudden arrival of the Stampede Marching Band, the louder arrival of an even larger symphonic orchestra, or the truly cacophonous arrival of several dozen cattle. Most of the perpetrators of these pranks were 50 or 60 years old (they're a lot older now) and they were having a heck of a time putting the dean down. In truth, though, I think they were rather glad to see me for they gave me my own cattle branding iron – one of two I have among my many prized mementos from those gatherings.

*"A business school must innovate and take risks, fail and try again."*

But our most innovative changes – as usual – came in our syllabi, in our curricula, in the way we taught. Many of the new developments took place at once – sometimes too quickly. I am first to admit, with the result that they were sometimes unreasonably abandoned. In 1964, we created a course on International Business. It was ahead of its time and lasted only two years. By 1975, however, the emerging importance of international business allowed us to resurrect our International Business Course in 1979 and we opened our Centre for International Business Studies, thanks in large part to Harold Crookell, who was instrumental in finding $160,000 worth of seed money. From the ashes of what appeared a failed course we have built an entire educational institute. A business school *must* innovate and take risks, fail, and try again if it is to sustain a commitment to excellence and keep not just apace but ahead of its times. Since 1964, faculty committees have reviewed every course the School has offered.

Our main difficulty, however, as the long range planning report of 1966 pointed out, was still faculty. We needed the best people and we needed a lot more of them. I began touring the U.S. in search of able minds, in particular Canadians who were studying in the United States. I traveled to Harvard, Wharton, MIT, Chicago, Indiana, UCLA, Berkeley, Stanford and Michigan, among others. Our other pressing need as a school was to get everyone pointed in more or less the same direction on what the School's goals and objectives were and how we could best realize them. We needed an organizational structure that would allow us to see them into place. It was out of this need to re-examine our fundamental

objectives that we began the long-standing series of retreats to the Caledon Club north of Toronto – and this in 1966, five to 10 years before 'think-sessions' became popular in the business community at large. But that is as it should be: if new ideas can't be tried and tested in a business school, where new ideas are the most valuable currency, where *can* they be tested?

*"We were always scrambling to make ends meet, somehow it made the entire job more satisfying."*

Changes continued apace. In 1966 we instituted a 'dynamic timetable' – dean-ese for a concept in scheduling whereby students learn certain material early in the term (say, planning and information control systems, or management science, or behavioral theories) in order that the same material can be used later in the term to teach different subjects (say Marketing and Finance, which these days in modern corporations are dependent on information control systems). That same term, Professor Andy Grindlay, one of our long-standing faculty members (who happens to hold his doctorate from UCLA) met the man who ran the Ford Motor Company's computers in Dearborn, Michigan. When the man from Ford told Andy the computers were unused at night, Andy reported back that he thought we might be able to use them provided we could get a telephone line into the facility. But a line cost money and the School didn't have any. Instead, we used our connections – which is an awful pun – and designed some training programs for Bell. In return, they ran a line from Western into Ford's Windsor, Ontario operation. We were always scrambling to make ends meet like that, and somehow it made the entire job a thousand times more satisfying. I guess it has to do with the size of your alligators.

And because everything happened at once, like a fine work of jazz, immense synergy occurred, particularly in the first year of our HBA and MBA Programs, where life was officially hell. Elsewhere student unrest prevailed. At the Business School, we advertised our summer programs in *TIME* magazine to enormous effect.

By 1969, we had spent our way through the Ford Foundation grant – but we still needed a computer centre that stayed open night and day. We were able to thank The Richard and Jean Ivey Foundation, once again, for its generosity in that regard. It was at roughly this time, too, that we introduced a series of experimental courses called Topics – any subject relevant to business provided it withstood a review after two years. Our pioneering course on Managing Change started out as a Topic.

Our students never hesitated to let us know how hard they were working. To my mind, the pattern has been the same over the years: each student feels boiler-like pressure his or her first year because we know what everyone's taking and we can apply the pressure evenly. By year two, students begin to pursue specific interests with the result that the pressure varies – or at least with the result that you must bear your pressure alone. We often tell students they will work harder in their two years at Western than they ever will in professional business life, and I honestly suspect that is true. But I pity the poor soul who finds himself saddled with Finance and Operations Management and Labor Relations in the same term. And everyone seems to complain still about Business Policy, the course in which teams of students go out and conduct a biopsy upon a living corporation and then present a prognosis to management. It continues to provide the glue for the entire School program because it is a course that marries the School's theoretical teaching to practical experience. And that, after all, is a lot of what the School is about.

*"As the School's Plan for Excellence emerged in the '70s our fund-raising goals shifted."*

As the School's Plan for Excellence emerged in the early 1970s, our fund-raising goals shifted. We wanted to finance more research, and develop more Canadian case problems for our students to examine. Thus the School witnessed the creation of the Associates Research Workshop. A radical idea, to say the least. The theory was that faculty from an array of universities could share research money to promote more synergy in research. We set up a Screening Committee to review applications: John Stenason, a member of our Advisory Committee, who holds a Ph.D. in Economics, was the Chairman. Then, to lubricate the source of the funds we held Associate Research Days in Montreal and Toronto. We were spending corporate money to fund research, why couldn't that research be explained in a language our benefactors would understand? One of the banks would donate a conference room and six or seven Western professors would share their research findings before a roomful of their corporate associates to explain where all their money was going. Out of the brain pan and into the fire was the popular expression for those sessions. We also hosted a series of research forums wherein business school faculty from institutions across the country could share their research findings with one another rather like an intellectual House of Commons, but with a smaller majority. We tried to foment national and international excitement for research on business practices – which, given our status as the flagship of Canadian business schools, struck me as a natural, responsible and, not incidentally, rather shrewd thing to do.

The conferences mathematically expanded our recruiting networks and exponentially swelled our storehouse of new ideas.

That year, as well, Andy Grindlay of our faculty created courses on The Manager and the Computer, while his colleague, Bert Wood, invented and directed a series of Production Operations Management Courses. Shortly thereafter I visited Max Murback, Director of Management and Training at the Ciba-Geigy Company in Switzerland, one of the world's largest drug companies and a former student of Bud Johnston's when Bud was teaching at Institut pour l'Étude des Méthodes de Dirèction de l'Entreprise (IMEDE) and Max informed me that Western's Production Management Course was considered the best in the world. By 1970, Western Business School faculty were teaching in England, Switzerland, Austria, France, Jamaica and Bermuda. That same year, Western's School of Business Administration published its first bibliography listing 400 Western cases. We began our Internship Program, which allowed HBA students to work for a term in the real world with real corporations as well as our Small Business Consulting Program which introduced students to small businesses and vice versa, and which in turn became the prototype for similar programs across the country. We were working hard. Our reputation was spreading, both at home and around the world. That seemed a sure sign of world-class excellence.

**"I think the emerging prominence of women represents a central virtue of the School. And that is our commitment to individual freedom...the underlying purpose is to create a society that in the end responsibly enlarges each individual's freedom."**

*"Without the vast generosity of our benefactors there would have been no computing, no research, no case materials, no fellowships to attract top people."*

The twin foundations of this commitment to excellence were our persistence as fund-raisers and the vast generosity of our benefactors. Without the latter, there would have been no computing, no Canadian case materials, no research, no fellowships to attract top people. Thanks to the efforts of our Advisory Committee and people such as Allan Burton (who became its Chairman in 1975-1976) and Bud Johnston, who was by that time Associate Dean, we were able to meet those commitments. Bud had already demonstrated his knack for planning by transforming our faculty retreats from 'thinkfests' into hard-edged review-and-planning sessions. I remember, too, the steady, quiet efforts of teachers such as Joe DiStefano and Allan Adlington, who developed the Senior University Administrators Course (SUAC) for university administrators who have not, traditionally, been trained as business executives.

All this effort by all these people yielded tangible results. In the 1977-1978 academic season, we enrolled 292 BAs, 438 MBAs and 35 Ph.Ds. We were approaching our optimal size and increasing quality, and faced greater competition from many more MBA Programs. We have had to limit enrollment since 1979. We have not, however, shirked our commitment to spreading the good management word through what my colleague Doreen Sanders, Editor and Publisher of *The Business Quarterly* aptly called 'the wider classroom'. Over the years we have created or taught courses or done both, for organizations as varied as the

Institute of Canadian Bankers, the Society of Industrial Cost Accountants, all levels of government, and even a Police College. In all there are 20 such outside courses.

The productivity of Western's School of Business Administration has grown phenomenally. I can say that with modesty for I am referring to the prodigious intellectual output of my colleagues. When I first set out into the world to visit corporations for advice and money, one research paper had been published out of our School. One paper! I photocopied it and proceeded to attach covers of different colored paper to make us look more productive. In 1987, just for comparative purposes, faculty at the School produced four books; a monograph; 38 journal articles; 78 case studies; and its annual bumper crop of Management Courses and regular academic activities. In the old days, being asked what we intended to do with the money was a tough question to answer: we had no previous record. It really makes my day to get asked the same question now in my peripatetic wanderings as a fund-raiser: I simply point to the glowing reputation of the School. For it is the final and incontrovertible proof not only that this School is first-class and world-class, but that we pulled ourselves up literally by the bootstraps. We had five professors in the early days. Now we have 75. Many have served for a long time.

I used to tell classes when they arrived that five of the 10 memorable teachers they would have in their lives would show up here at the School. That's a very strong statement, but I'd make it again today with much less hesitation. As I read over the record of this School's past, I am reminded again and again of its preoccupation, its obsession with results. *Results* have been the reason we always put the

education of our students ahead of faculty research – a silent rule, I might add, that no dean could ever impose or enforce but which is the cornerstone of Western's Business School. It is important to teach and to be able to teach in order to survive at this School. We tell it to everyone who comes here. Not everyone remembers, and not everyone makes it.

It demands commitment on the part of our students too. More and more it will depend upon a commitment from students at the doctoral level. Our emphasis on teaching has meant that our commitment to research, while laudable, has been a part-time one. I feel we must now move to the next step, to develop full-time research programs. The need for a deeper, broader and more conceptual understanding of management and the workings of business are made painfully clear throughout society every day. I think we have taken the first step in our efforts to strengthen our Doctoral Program. I can see results shining just up ahead. We're a good school now, and I am proud to say I helped make us one. But we have the potential now, under the leadership of new men, to be a truly great school. Of course, my colleagues are always telling me I'm the most optimistic fellow in the world. I remind them that they thought I was crazy years ago too, when I used to tell them Western's School of Business Administration was going to be the national business school of Canada. They laughed at me. Old Jack, what an imagination. Today we are *the* national business school in Canada. A fifth of our MBA class comes from Winnipeg and points west; our Management Courses attract applicants from coast to coast. My colleagues have themselves to thank for the responsibility their reputation entails.

No small part of the School's achievements is due to what I see in retrospect as our rather progressive and forward-looking approach to communications and improving the public image of business.

Dr. D. Carlton Williams, Western's President (1967-1976) adds the University's congratulations to *The Business Quarterly* on the occasion of its 40th anniversary while Dean Wettlaufer and Doreen Sanders (Editor/Publisher 1961-1988) respond to his remarks.

into my office and said, "I think you should see this." In her hand she held the newly redesigned cover of *The Quarterly* – a beautiful painting by Greg Curnoe of London festooned with a stamped slogan that read "Impotent Canadians always prostrate themselves to the United States." Well…hell. The bulk of my corporate associates were Americans. And yet here was this painting, with its anti-American slogan, right across the cover of the flagship publication of the School. "Doreen," I said, "can't we get this on the second or third issue of the new *Quarterly*?"

"No, Jack," she said, with her usual sweet smile and eminently reasonable tone of voice. "Greg Curnoe, the artist, was told it would be on this one. And, if we don't publish it he plans to organize a group of artists to march on the campus with signs reading "The Western Business School does not believe in freedom for artists to express themselves."

What could I say? There were a few letters as a result. But, more importantly, an important and courageous principle, the freedom of expression at Western's Business School, was upheld.

---

### *"I think the emerging prominence of women represents a central virtue of the School…"*

---

The subject of women at the School of Business Administration is an interesting and delicate one. For many years the School had a terrible time attracting women, particularly into the MBA Program. It was never just a matter of being able to find jobs for women once they graduated: our female graduates were enormously qualified. The paradox was that there was no network for our female graduates to exploit, no skein of women graduates who had risen to positions of corporate prominence. A network is essential to an MBA Program. In

The challenge facing the School of Business in the early 1950s and 1960s, and even today, has consisted not only of creating Canadian case materials and establishing the School's presence in both the academic and the business community, but of establishing Canadian business as a subject worthy of study and respect. That may seem hard to believe in these business-conscious times when capitalism is well regarded, but I assure you the business world was no one's favorite son when I took over as Dean of Business at Western. No small part of the credit for establishing the respectability of business as a legitimate intellectual and societal concern in Canada must go to Doreen Sanders, who for the

last 12 years has been the Editor and Publisher of *The Business Quarterly*, and who transformed it from an impoverished fledgling publication into the country's preeminent business journal.

I first met Doreen when she was one of my students in Business 20: she had a Jaguar then, and the impression the car made on campus was only intensified when fashionable Doreen stepped from its driver's seat. I well remember the first cover of *The Business Quarterly* on which she wanted to reproduce an original Canadian work of art – something that had never been done in Canadian business magazines, but which is now much-copied. I was Dean, and as usual in the midst of a delicate fund-raising drive. Doreen stepped my first year as Dean, there were four women in the class. I became concerned enough about that meager number to write a letter to the presidents of Canada's 150 largest companies. I pointed out that I considered it most important that women ought to begin to flow back through our professional management courses, in order to prime the ground for increasing numbers of women entering the School as full-time students. I am saddened to say that I received some extraordinary replies. One, from a senior executive I will refrain from identifying, went on at great length about how and why women in business were not his first priority. I wasn't surprised, shortly thereafter, when he landed himself in a flaming public controversy over the subject of women on his board – and ended up with some women elected to his board anyway. Tradition dies hard not in business per se, but – as Dickens might have said – only within the petrified heads of individuals. Thanks in large part to the efforts of Bud Johnston, who has resisted artificial and ghettoizing measures such as affirmative action programs, women accounted for nearly 30% of the MBA class in 1984-1985.

---

**"The School is a company of intellectual entrepreneurs and mental adventurers."**

---

I think the emerging prominence of women represents a central virtue of the School of Business here at Western. And that is our commitment to individual freedom. I have often asked myself why I liked the job I had, and why my colleagues and I enjoy working here in an environment that is 'about business', rather than within it. The cynical reply is always that those who can do, while those who can't, teach – but that is, as I say, the cynical reply. I believe the reason has more to do with freedom, with the opportunity this job offers to

continue to build one's intellectual capital. It lets Jack Wettlaufer be Jack Wettlaufer. This School is a company of intellectual entrepreneurs, of mental adventurers. The School goes out of its way to make its courses as dependable as possible, to unify programs and procedures as much as we can for the sake of efficiency. We train our students in standard procedures where they are applicable, and we emphasize the importance of a team to any creative administrative effort. But the collective effort is doomed to fail unless its underlying purpose is to create a society that in the end responsibly enlarges each individual's freedom. That, I like to hope, is what this School of Business has always been at heart: a society, an intellectual civilization, a collection of individual ideas, hopes, worries, efforts and dreams.

Back in my university days, I used to race motorcycles. A Harley-Davidson, to be precise, in the late 1940s, after the war. I was pretty good, but the race I remember best was a 100 mile marathon in which I placed fifth. I remember it not because fifth is anything to remember, but because the guy who came in sixth was a fellow named Goldsmith who the next year went on to win the U.S. National Championships. I've always felt proud of that; I never won the big race everyone talked about, but I knew I was at least as good as the man who did. My point is not to laud my motorcycle riding abilities, of course, but to make an analogy. For a long time, Western's School of Business Administration enjoyed the same sense of self-awareness: we weren't perceived to be a winner, but we knew we were as good as the winners, as good as any other school. I think we have proven that, the challenge now is to go on to lead. To be a leader, like most of the difficult jobs in life,

requires courage. We will only achieve it if we continue to emphasize teaching, if we continue to make what we teach challenging and exciting. We will only achieve it if we remember what it is that makes a business school distinct from the business world it invariably serves and leads: that it is a grouping of colleagues and equals when the freedom to think whatever it is necessary to think is of paramount and eternal importance. No grant, no gift, no research foundation, no consulting contract, no international centre, no reward, no personal relationship can be allowed to threaten that fragile freedom. Ironically, I think freedom is appreciated most of all by anyone who has had the good fortune to attend a great school, which is why so many of our graduates remember their days at Western fondly. We work together, *with* each other, rather than *for* someone else. I think too that the need for this freedom, even within existing corporations, will become more and more an issue with time, especially as vast numbers of highly-motivated post-war children come of age in the modern corporation and discover that there are only so many executive offices at the top of the corporate pyramid.

---

**"While Dean I witnessed one of the most significant developments of this century: the humanization of capitalism."**

---

In the period of time during which I was Dean of this School, I witnessed what I believe will come to be seen as one of the most significant developments of this century: namely, the humanization of capitalism. I say this notwithstanding the many great advances, technological and otherwise, that have changed the way business is done. More than ever, business is an artful science and a scientific art. Executives have had to become more and more expert at a host of tasks. It is, we have to admit, more than ever a science. And yet it is more than ever, as Walter Thompson once described it, a 'judgment art' as well. It is, finally, the practice of human beings, not of machines and abstract precepts. I think we do well to remember that fact at a time when computerization and its brother, specialization, dominate our thinking and occasionally threaten to shrink the scale of our thoughts so small that they become invisible to the human eye. There is no such thing, as Dickens again remarked, as bad capitalism; there are only bad capitalists. And Dickens and I aren't alone in noticing the fact. Many years ago now, in 1957, I heard Stanley Teele, then Dean of the Harvard Business School, deliver a remarkable speech upon receiving an honorary degree from Western. His words stay with me to this day:

> "A man's personal philosophy, his way of looking at the world, and the men and women around him, determine his success as a manager of things and people more than any other single factor. His basic attitudes are far more significant than the technique he uses. As we learn more and more about the business organization as a social unit, we have become increasingly certain that the executive's skill with people – or the lack of it – is the determining element in his long range success or failure. As we look ahead, we have reason to believe that this will be increasingly true. In short, the time may come when an evil man, or one who has no clear sense of values, simply cannot be an administrator."

It is in assessing the role of business in a turbulent, increasingly angry and yet interdependent world (a world where rain in Harare affects the rate of inflation in Toronto) that we will most of all need our resources of

"Back in my university days, I used to race motorcycles. A Harley-Davidson, to be precise, in the late 1940s, after the war...I never won the big race everyone talked about, but I knew I was at least as good as the man who did...I had beaten him previously in a 100 mile marathon. My point is not to laud my motorcycle riding abilities, but to make an analogy..."

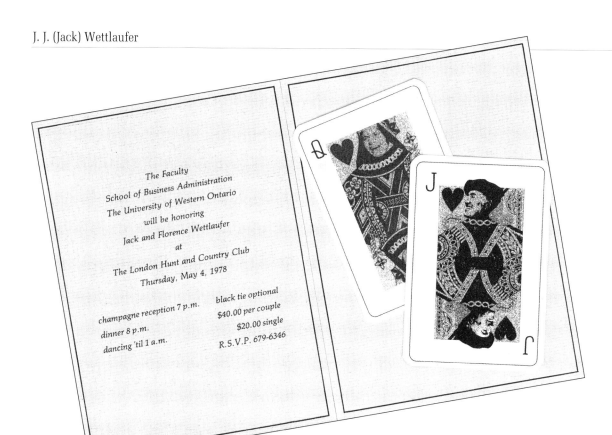

The Faculty
School of Business Administration
The University of Western Ontario
will be honoring
Jack and Florence Wettlaufer
at
The London Hunt and Country Club
Thursday, May 4, 1978

champagne reception 7 p.m.     black tie optional
dinner 8 p.m.                  $40.00 per couple
dancing 'til 1 a.m.            $20.00 single
                               R.S.V.P. 679-6346

"The Queen and Jack of Hearts" was the theme of the party given for the Wettlaufers on the occasion of Jack's retirement as Dean. During the evening, a film directed by C.B. (Bud) Johnston and produced by faculty and staff, was shown. Titled *"Thanks Jack!"* it was a fun-filled tribute to Jack. Following his retirement, he continued to teach and was Ambassador for the School in all aspects of fund-raising. Following his death in 1992, the newly completed Executive Development Centre, established by Western Business School in Mississauga, Ontario was named in his honor.

judgment. How will we defeat the scourge of protectionism? How can we best assist in the economic development of the Third World without being colonialists on the one hand, negligent on the other? How will we readjust the international financial system so as to avoid another banking crisis – provided the current one doesn't finish us off first? How can we – as I feel we must – begin to account for unemployment and retraining as a cost of doing business? How much autonomy in our financial and personal lives are we willing to relinquish to government intervention? Should a corporation be more accountable for the morality of its investment decisions. Or is there merit in letting businesses be morally neutral? Writing in *The McKinsey Quarterly,* in an essay entitled "A New Look At Corporate Responsibility," Peter Drucker, the management consultant, noted that "in the next decade it will become increasingly important to stress that business can discharge its social responsibilities only if it converts them into self-interest. That is, into business opportunity." We will do that, and pay heed to Stanley Teele's wisdom, only if we train our future capitalists well.

---

*"Napoleon was right when he said we do much better to consult our hopes rather than our fears."*

---

Unfortunately, there are no set rules as to how we can best accomplish this goal, just as there are no answers to the genuinely troubling economic questions we must ask and address and, if we can, answer in our time. There are only alternative courses of action, recommendations and the unpredictable future. If it lies anywhere we can reach, the future of capitalism, and perhaps with it a good part of the future of western civilization, lies as always in human character – for it is personalities, and not principles, that move an age. It is personalities we bend and mold here at the School of Business Administration of The University of Western Ontario. Twenty-five years ago when I was made Dean of this School, I knew only one thing: that I was determined to have a good school. I had few rational reasons to believe we could achieve that successfully, and even fewer to support my conviction that one day this would be the best business school in Canada. Which only goes to show that Napoleon was right when he said we do much better to consult our hopes rather than our fears.

## J. J. WETTLAUFER

During the October 29th, 1967 Annual Autumn Convocation ceremonies at Waterloo Lutheran University, Waterloo, Ontario, The Honorable W. Ross Macdonald, Chancellor, conferred the degree of Doctor of Laws, *honoris causa,* to Dean Wettlaufer. The citation reads as follows:

*John Jacob Wettlaufer, Dean of the School of Business Administration at The University of Western Ontario, began his education at Waterloo College, then continued to his present school, completing work for his bachelor's degree in Honors Business Administration in 1950. A year later he received his Master's degree and was invited to join the faculty.*

*His contribution as a teacher and administrator, and his great ability to communicate effectively, resulted in his swift recognition within the School. In 1962, he was chosen for the position of Associate Dean and a year later he was elevated to Dean. His services have found wide application throughout Canadian and international business. He has been called upon as a researcher and consultant by business firms, and has assisted the Stanford Research Institute in California, the staff college of the*

*Canadian National Railways, the management program for Pakistan, and the National Productivity Council.*

*Dean Wettlaufer has been Director of the Marketing Management Course since its inception in 1953. He serves as a member of the Board of Governors of the Institute of Canadian Bankers and the Co-ordinating and Advisory Committee of the Ontario Department of Education. In addition, he is the co-author of the definitive text, Business Administration in Canada, published in 1962.*

*But Dean Wettlaufer's concerns are not restricted to the field of business. He is Chairman of the Evangelism Committee and member of the Church Council of Redeemer Lutheran Church, London, and will be a delegate to the 1968 Atlanta convention of the Lutheran Church in America. In addition, Dean Wettlaufer is Chairman of the Lutheran Campus Foundation of Ontario, and is a former member of the Board of Governors of Waterloo Lutheran University. During the Second World War, he was an active member of the armed forces at home and overseas.*

*Dean Wettlaufer has given distinguished leadership to every task that has engaged his attention. He exemplifies the finest qualities as citizen, churchman, educator and author.*

# Expanding the vision

*The 1980s saw an accelerated rate of change in the issues facing management and the technologies available to address them. Accordingly, the School under the energetic leadership of C.B. (Bud) Johnston, responded by focusing on, among other topics, the globalization of business, developments in computers and information systems and the importance of dealing effectively with governments. Part of his vision was to establish a national centre for management research and development. Its mandate would be to catalyze and assist in funding business research at Western and at other Canadian business schools and to disseminate research findings to practicing managers and academics. The National Centre for Management Research and Development became a reality in 1986. In this chapter, written in 1992-93, he recounts how, during his tenure as dean, he expanded the ambitions of his predecessors and established new goals to meet the changing times.*

It was late June of 1975. My wife, Carol, and I were in Lausanne, Switzerland where I was finishing teaching a three-week Marketing Course for IMEDE (now IMD). The phone rang and it was Jack Wettlaufer calling from Canada indicating he would be in Geneva the following Saturday and inviting us to have lunch with him. We accepted of course, only to learn, over lunch, that he had made the trip expressly to offer me the position of Associate Dean at the School. Nick Fry had completed a term as Associate Dean and would return to outstanding teaching in our Degree and Executive Programs, and to giving strong leadership in the Business Policy area.

Jack's offer came as a complete surprise. Although I had, during my 18 years on the faculty, held a number of administrative positions such as Director of our Marketing Management and Management Training Courses for executives, and Chairman of the Undergraduate and Continuing Education Programs, I had never considered joining the office of the dean. Carol and I took a short holiday in the south of France to think over the implications of such an appointment. By the end of the following week I had confirmed my acceptance.

For the next three years I learned from Jack, John Graham, our Assistant Dean – Administration, and other members of the institution, the rudiments of managing the School. In 1978, on Jack's retirement and after the traditional university search for a dean, I was offered the job.

My greatest misgiving in accepting the deanship was filling the enormous shoes of my predecessor. As Dean for the previous 15 years, Jack Wettlaufer had built the School on solid foundations and extended its reputation nationwide. Although much opportunity remained, his would be a very tough act to follow. Nonetheless, the resources were there to build further, the most important of which was a highly committed and capable faculty and staff and a well-developed culture that differentiated Western, in several important dimensions, from most other business schools.

Among the more important aspects of the School's culture was an extraordinary commitment to excellence in teaching by the case method and the development of our students' analytical, decision-making and implementation skills as practicing general managers – not just as students of business or narrow, functional specialists. Throughout all our programs the emphasis was heavily on the development of student insights and talents. Unlike the lecture method of teaching in which the intellectual competence of the faculty is apparent, the case method also requires the teacher's orchestration of the students' inputs so as to provide a unique learning experience, not just the display of faculty expertise. It was made clear to new recruits to the faculty that "if you couldn't teach, you couldn't stay."

Our pervasive use of the case method, rather than the lecture method, in pursuing these teaching goals was expensive and demanding, requiring constant investment in new and updated case materials. The process of case writing has the great advantage, however, of keeping faculty in touch with practicing managers and emerging issues. New cases add excitement and relevance to the classroom experience for our students.

The School's focus on developing students as general managers resulted in ongoing efforts to offer an integrated program rather than just a set of isolated courses. Professors regularly referred to issues and ideas developed in other classes by their teaching colleagues thus encouraging students to think across course lines. During their first year in the School, students in both the HBA and MBA Programs were organized into sections of 65-70, and taught a full set of required courses, in the

---

**"Increasingly, we recognize the need for effective management in all aspects of society's affairs."**

*"As The University of Western Ontario prepares to enter its second century, I am sure you are aware that the challenges ahead are formidable indeed, not only for universities, but also for the country as a whole. Increasingly, we are coming to recognize the need for effective management in all aspects of society's affairs.*

*That the manager's job is changing will not be news to any of you. The complex ramifications of key decisions have to be made in a world of greater uncertainty, demand a higher degree of professional competence than ever before – competence not only in terms of technical capability, but also increasingly in sensitivity to and ability to deal with the many environmental factors that figure so prominently in the longer range consequences*

*of action taken today.*

*Fundamentally committed to the task of developing managers with a high degree of skill in analysis and action-oriented decision-making, the School continues to strive towards fulfilling that responsibility at an increasing standard of excellence.*

*Vitally important to that task are our efforts to develop new teaching materials and to undertake research on issues of importance to today's and tomorrow's thoughtful practitioners of the art.*

*Without the support and co-operation of our alumni and other friends of the School in key positions in both the public and private sectors across the country we would have been unable to achieve the level of success we have and on which we can continue to build.*
– C.B. Johnston writing for
*Western Management Magazine* in 1978.

---

same classroom, by a consistent group of seven, or so, faculty who met regularly to review their section's progress across the entire curriculum. This allowed dynamic time-tabling sequenced in such a way as to permit courses to build on each other. During the final year, students were free to choose from among a wide range of elective courses but were required to take the full-year course in Business Policy integrating all functions of a business from a general management point of view. As part of Business Policy, students completed a major field project in which they were required to report their

findings to managers of the companies they were studying. Since 1980, a half-course in the Political Environment of Business, originally, based on Don Thain's earlier work in Business Government Relations, was also required.

The recruitment and development of faculty was of key concern. I was constantly amazed that potential faculty recruits, visiting with us, returned to my office to relate that all the faculty members they had visited had described the School, its values and expectations of colleagues, in basically the same way.

The institution knew what it was and what it wasn't; who it wanted as colleagues and who it didn't.

It was critical that those we invited to join the faculty shared our concept of the School and its high commitment to teaching as well as research. Candidates with those characteristics were few and far between and in strong demand by other outstanding schools – particularly in the U.S. Together with the associates deans, I made a practice of traveling to visit many faculty prospects on their home grounds to personally present our offers to them and their spouses, usually over dinner.

Among the recruiting successes of which I am particularly proud was our ability to attract the future Dean, Adrian Ryans, back to the School from his position on the Stanford faculty. Another rare success lay in persuading the Honorable Gordon Osbaldeston, O.C., P.C., and a 1953 graduate of our MBA Program, to join us after a full career as Canada's senior civil servant. In addition to teaching alongside Harold Crookell in the Political Environment of Business Course, Gordon authored two definitive works on organization and management in government.

---

*"Absolutely fundamental to the School's success, since its establishement as a separate faculty in 1949, has been the role of the Advisory Committee – we owe a deep debt of gratitude to those who have given their time and effort in encouraging and supporting the School's development."*

---

Since its establishment as a separate faculty in 1949, the Western Business School has benefited from the counsel of its Advisory Committee comprised of roughly 35 senior executives of Canadian companies from across the country or their equivalent in government as well as several senior University officials.

The *Plan for Excellence,* a creation of the Advisory Committee to attract corporate support primarily for research and case writing, proved to be absolutely fundamental to the School's success. It had been recognized early that we could not expect to build and operate a first-class institution on government and tuition funding alone. Additional, continuing, financial support would be critical. The Advisory Committee's role in the success of these efforts proved invaluable.

During my tenure, I worked with four chairmen of the Committee: Alan Burton of Simpsons, Jack Armstrong of Imperial Oil, Ralph Barford of GSW and Camco, and Don Campbell of Maclean Hunter. Each of these men, in their own way, acted as a sounding-board for the School's proposed undertakings and supported me strongly on my presentation of these ideas for Committee comment and advice. We owe a deep debt of gratitude to these gentlemen and their Committee colleagues for their time and effort in encouraging and supporting the School's further development.

Throughout my 11 years as Dean, I was very fortunate to have been able to attract the direct assistance of five very capable and very supportive associate deans. As I learned during my three years in that position under Jack Wettlaufer, the increasing demands on the dean from fund-raising and other outside activities, resulted in more and more of the internal management tasks falling to the associate dean. David Shaw accepted my offer of that position and very capably handled a tremendous workload, including the pro-tem chairmanship of the HBA and Ph.D Programs at different points, in his three-year term from 1978 to 1981.

In 1981, I accepted a Faculty Advisory Committee recommendation to appoint two

**"The School's focus is on developing students as general managers, not narrow, functional specialists."**

"John Nicholson gave early leadership to the HBA Program which came to be embraced by students and faculty as probably one of the finest, undergraduate business education experiences anywhere in the world."

Fewer than half of these students were headed for the Business School. The courses had developed such positive reputations that many students, on other career paths, saw them as appropriate for their ambitions as well and this reflected handsomely on the Business School within the University community.

The Honors Business Administration Program annually admitted only 145-150 outstanding undergraduates, who had completed the first two years of university to spend the final two years of that four-year program entirely at the Business School. Chaired by John Nicholson, Dave Peach, Jim Erskine and subsequently Ken Hardy, the program was enthusiastically embraced by the students and faculty alike as probably one of the finest undergraduate business education experiences anywhere in the world.

To maintain the quality of this experience, we continually resisted pressure from the University administration to expand the size of the program to levels of undergraduate programs in most other schools.

In 1981, the HBA Council proposed offering a one-day conference to which senior business executives would be invited to address the students. The proposal received enthusiastic support from the School and was a resounding success. It has been continued every year since then, entirely student organized and operated.

Consistent with the recommendations of an earlier established Long-Range Planning Committee headed by Don Thain, the two-year MBA Program was the School's largest, admitting, each year, 250 or so, students from coast to coast in Canada and about 10% from overseas. Successively chaired during this period by Blair Little, Peter Newson, Larry Wynant and Jim Rush, the program was Canada's only truly national MBA Program as recruiting efforts across the country in search of the best students paid off.

associate deans. Al Mikalachki accepted the appointment as Associate Dean – Programs, a position he held until his appointment as Acting Dean on my stepping down in 1989. Joe DiStefano took on the job of Associate Dean – Human Resources, as did David Peach and Terry Deutscher, for subsequent terms. Managing a faculty in a university has been likened to 'herding cats' and each of these men brought to the job their own particularly effective style of managing their delicate, demanding and often difficult task.

The greatest pleasure of my job was working with these men and other members of the faculty and staff, as we continued to expand and extend the School's influence on management practice.

Throughout the 1980s our Degree Programs continued to flourish. Under the chairmanship of John Humphrey, followed by Rich Mimick and John Graham, Pre-Business offered one course to each of the freshman and sophomore students throughout the University. At one point Business 20 was drawing close to half the roughly 4,000 freshmen and Business 257, 20% to 25% of the sophomore registrants.

**The National Centre for Management Research and Development, Western Business School.**

The accomplishments and assistance of our alumni were important factors in our ability to attract the number and quality of applicants we enjoyed. In 1975, Jack and I, with the help of key alumni, organized the first Western Business School Club in Toronto, a model for other clubs later established in Montreal, Ottawa, Kitchener-Waterloo, London, Winnipeg, Regina, Calgary, Edmonton and Vancouver. In 1986, we set up our first club outside Canada with the enthusiastic help of alumni in Hong Kong.

Student exchange programs with schools in other countries, begun in 1978 with the London Business School in the U.K., had grown by 1988 to include schools in The Netherlands, Belgium, France, Spain, Sweden, Germany, Hong Kong and Japan, adding an ever-increasing international dimension to the program.

Carol and I annually held receptions at our home for students from other countries and cultures as we did for faculty and staff at Christmas until that group became too large for us to accommodate.

The 1980s saw an accelerated rate of change in the issues facing management and the technologies available to address these issues. Accordingly, the MBA curriculum was modified and updated regularly to include increased content focusing on, among others, the globalization of business, developments in computers and information systems and the importance of dealing effectively with governments in business affairs. Changes in the MBA Program consistently filtered through to the HBA Program, enriching it as well.

The Ph.D Program, committed primarily to producing teachers of business, and which had developed slowly throughout the 1960s and 1970s, reached new levels of output. Chairmen Bob Britney, Blair Little and Chris Haehling von Lanzenauer promoted the program strongly to potential candidates and to the faculty and ably assisted candidates in accessing sources of government and private funding support. The late 1980s saw total enrollments grow to 40, or more, students at one stage or another of completion. Since admission was closely screened and candidates were not required to serve extensively as research or teaching assistants, Western's completion rate of 70% to 80% remained exceptionally high.

During this period, the School's program of project and case research was chaired by Al Mikalachki, Terry Deutscher and Jim Hatch. The aim of responsible spending of the *Plan for Excellence* funds for these purposes prompted each of these chairmen to closely manage the program focusing on research initiatives with high scholarly standards, but also of strong interest to practising managers.

To support our heavy investment in case writing and in response to interest from other schools, Jim Erskine and Mike Leenders annually offered their courses in case writing and case teaching at Western and, over time, in more than 20 other countries as far flung as Argentina, Pakistan, Spain and Singapore.

---

***The idea of a centre for management research was first suggested by Johnston in 1978 – in 1986 it became a reality with the completion of the building – on time and on budget.***

---

By the late 1970s, it was becoming increasingly evident that additional faculty time, space and funding would be required if the School was to increase its contribution to the practice of management through research. Because of our

heavy commitment to teaching and teaching materials development, research had not captured a large portion of our resources. Funding from our *Plan for Excellence* had proved to be invaluable support for case writing, and such research as we did undertake, but the level of research activity would have to be increased if we were to maintain the School's intellectual vitality and attract the best faculty.

The general idea of a research centre was first presented to the University Administration as a long-term goal as part of our 1978 five-year plan but, since funding was not likely to be available through the University at that time, it was not until 1983 that the work began, in earnest, to make such a centre a reality. In the spring of 1983, President George Connell called at about 11:30 one morning to advise us he had just received a call from the federal government representing the ministries of Finance and Science and Technology, inquiring about projects in the value of $5 to $10 million that they might consider funding prior to the upcoming election.

Aware of our management research centre ambitions, George suggested that we call the government back by 3:30 that afternoon, as they had requested, to get their preliminary reaction to our basic ideas. After a few hours of very intensive planning, we called back only to learn later that their priorities for this request focused on more 'hard science' projects and that our proposal would not qualify in this round of consideration. They were, nonetheless, very supportive of our concept and encouraged us to pursue funding through other branches of the federal government. Subsequent exploration produced little of promise in terms of government programs that could accommodate a project of the size and nature that we were proposing.

In February 1984, I received a call from the Honorable Ed Lumley, then Minister of the Department of Regional and Industrial

Expansion (DRIE), inquiring about the appropriateness of our MBA Program for his son Bob, who was completing his undergraduate degree at the University of Ottawa. I had gotten to know Ed Lumley some

"I returned to my office which was filled waist-high with balloons, a bottle of champagne and the door papered over with 'Congratulations'. It was the warmest welcome I had ever received. The NCMRD was to become a reality."

years earlier when, as the Coca-Cola bottler in Cornwall, he had attended an executive development program we had run for the Canadian company. Since I was planning to be in Ottawa the following week, I offered to meet with Bob separately, as was my custom, and inquired as to whether it might be appropriate for Ed and me to meet subsequently insofar as I had a proposal he might find interesting. Such a meeting was arranged and attended also by Gordon Ritchie, Associate Deputy Minister, who would subsequently lead me through the many intricacies of preparing a proposal for government approval.

Ed Lumley liked our ideas, as did his colleagues, and I was given the go-ahead at the meeting to prepare a detailed proposal in which the government could be expected to provide one-third of the funding with the balance to be raised from the University and the private sector. The Minister cautioned that, since a cabinet shuffle would probably occur in late June, approval by the government should be completed by early that month. In the ensuing hectic three months, we received enthusiastic support from the faculty, the University and our Advisory Committee.

*"Ralph Barford, then Chairman of the Advisory Committee, admitted later that he "wondered what I'd been smoking" when I first introduced the broad idea in a meeting with him shortly after my return from Ottawa."*

Ralph Barford, then Chairman of the Advisory Committee, admitted later that he "wondered what I'd been smoking" when I first introduced the broad idea in a meeting with him shortly after my return from Ottawa. Both he and

David S.R. Leighton (left), first Director of NCMRD (1987-1991), and Donald H. Thain, colleagues since their student-days at Harvard, have made an important contribution to Canadian business through their extensive research program on corporate governance and boards of directors.

President George Connell, however, provided strong support for the proposal when it was brought before the Advisory Committee for approval to go forward.

After innumerable meetings at the School, and trips to Ottawa, to avail myself of the invaluable advice of ministry officials on how best to frame the proposal and speed it through the approval stages, a final draft of an agreement was completed and jointly signed in Ottawa during the first week of June, in record time, we were told.

The federal government would provide $4.2 million towards the cost of the $12.2 million project, and the University $3 million leaving $5 million to be raised from the private sector. The Advisory Committee had committed $1.5 million from the School's *Plan for Excellence* private sector funding and $3.5

million would have to come from other sources.

I returned to my office the afternoon of the signing to find the door papered over with a message reading "Congratulations" and the office filled, waist-high, with multi-colored balloons and a bottle of champagne on my desk. Faculty and staff had spent much of the morning blowing up the balloons for the warmest welcome home I had ever received. The National Centre for Management Research and Development would become a reality.

The Centre's mandate would be to catalyze and assist in funding business research at Western and at other Canadian business schools and to disseminate research findings to practicing managers and other academics through publications, executive development courses and degree programs. Research, at the outset, would concentrate on entrepreneurship, productivity and international business. Other topics such as women in management, generating profits from new technology, doing business in the U.S. and corporate governance would be addressed as interest and funding allowed.

In searching for a director of the Centre, we felt fortunate to have David Leighton agree to return to the School in 1985 to serve in that capacity for the Centre's first five years. David had left the faculty in the early 1970s to build the Banff Centre into a world-recognized institution and had subsequently served terms as President and CEO of the Calgary Olympic Committee and Chairman of Nabisco Brands Ltd. Canada.

Our Building Committee of Terry Deutscher, Mike Leenders and Nancy Graham, assisted, latterly, by David Leighton and throughout by Russ Gonder, head of the University's Department of Physical Plant, oversaw the design and completion of the 37,500 square foot addition to the School. The building opened in September of 1986, on time and on budget.

To attract the required private sector support for the NCMRD and the School, the concept of funded professorships was established in 1985 with a price tag attached of $500,000 in endowed funding or $50,000, per year, for a ten-year period.

David Leighton and I were able to attract senior support of this magnitude from Magna International Inc., Nabisco Brands Ltd., The Imperial Life Assurance Company, Royal Bank of Canada and Hewlett-Packard (Canada) Ltd. Ralph Barford established a Professorship to honor his father, R.A. Barford, a prominent advertising and media executive. Maclean Hunter Ltd. supported a Professorship in the name of Donald F. Hunter, fourth Chief Executive of

Maclean Hunter (1964-1970) and Chairman (1970-1976). In 1989, The Canada Trust Company honored J. Allyn Taylor, President (1968-1973) and Chairman (1973-1978) and Arthur H. Mingay, Chairman (1979-1985), by funding the School's first endowed Chair in their names, in the amount of $1.5 million.

Additional funding was forthcoming for the NCMRD on David Leighton's initiative and, by 1987, we had reached our private sector support objectives as originally set out.

---

*"The Richard Ivey Foundation and The Richard and Jean Ivey Fund had generously funded the purchase of our first computer mainframe and terminals in 1969."*

---

The constraints of our computing capacity for teaching, research and administrative purposes became vividly clear in the late 1970s. The Richard Ivey Foundation and The Richard and Jean Ivey Fund had generously funded the purchase of our first computer mainframe and terminals in 1969. Recognizing the technical advances in the field and the increasing potential for the use of computers in management, The Richard Ivey Foundation again funded the purchase of a new and larger computing facility and the establishment of The Richard G. Ivey Computing Centre in the School in 1979, as well as further upgrading of the Centre's capacity in 1982.

In the spring of 1984, we were able to establish an additional student computer lab with the support of Hewlett-Packard (Canada) Ltd.'s donation of 20 personal computers for student use. Four years later, Hewlett-Packard upgraded this installation with improved models of personal computers, printers and software.

Mrs. R.M. (Beryl) Ivey (left), and Mrs. Lorraine Shuttleworth, shown here at the opening of The Richard G. Ivey Computing Centre, have long been benefactors as, early on, they recognized the technical advances in the field and the increasing potential for the use of computers in management.

In the early fall of 1984, Alan Adlington, in his capacity as the University's Acting President and Vice-Chancellor, and I, visited IBM Canada Ltd. to explain the School's activities and to elicit the company's support of our ambitions. IBM's response was encouraging but vague at the time, but a few months later I received a call asking if an IBM team could visit the School to explore our operations in depth. The visit would be part of a preliminary investigation of the possibility that the company would supply us, under its Corporate and Scientific Program, with a large quantity of computing equipment and software to establish a model business school computing facility for teaching and research. In return, the School would have to commit to developing, over a three-year period, a set of 'deliverables' in

**Alan Adlington (left), the University's Acting President and Vice-Chancellor is seen here, in 1985, with John M. Thompson, President of IBM Canada, signing a $3 million agreement that, through IBM's Corporate and Scientific Program, provided the School with a large quantity of computing equipment and software thus establishing a model business school computing facility for teaching and research.**

development needs of technology-based businesses.

Executive programs, like other products, go through life cycles and regularly have to be revitalized, and, in some cases, phased out as they come to the end of their useful existence. In 1976, Joe DiStefano had established Canada's first Senior University Administrators' Course with support from The Kellogg Foundation and The Richard and Jean Ivey Fund. Although very successful under Joe's and later John Kennedy's direction, this program was transferred to the University of Manitoba after more than 10 years of operation as other faculty priorities developed and demanded faculty attention. Similarly, the Management for Accounting and Financial Executives Course, which had earlier thrived under Ross Archibald's direction, and several other experimental program ventures were phased out as markets and faculty priorities shifted.

terms of an expanded student lab facility, new and enhanced courses and teaching materials, research on computer applications in management, publications and conferences for other business schools across the country.

During the ensuing months our faculty team of Sid Huff, Chris Piper and Bob White determined and negotiated our requirements and commitments. With strong staff support from Nancy Graham, Steve Moss and Helen Tomlinson, the system was installed in 1985, including a 4381 mainframe, 40 terminals, 101 personal computers, peripheral hardware and software and a local area network in the value of $3 million, the largest such project that IBM had funded to that time and the only one in a Canadian business school. The deliverables were completed, and in June 1988, IBM granted title to the equipment and software to the University.

The fourth decade of executive education at Western, beginning in 1978, was one of

experimentation and growth. The Management Training Course, established in 1948 under Walter Thompson's direction, continued to thrive as did the Marketing Management Course under Dave Burgoyne's leadership. The Production/Operations Management Course, founded by Bert Wood and one of the few programs of its type anywhere, regularly attracted a number of participants from around the world. Harold Crookell's founding and direction of the International Management Course, in 1978, resulted in classes in which roughly half the participants were from outside Canada. The Senior Managers' Program, founded in 1983 and directed by Nick Fry to focus on-top level corporate strategy, drew a more senior executive than we had attracted earlier. In 1988, Adrian Ryans established the highly focused, up-market Executive Marketing Program to address the specific management

**"Shortly after my appointment as Dean, Dave Burgoyne very capably took over my earlier role as Chairman of Continuing Education..."**

Shortly after my appointment as Dean, Dave Burgoyne very capably took over my earlier role as Chairman of Continuing Education until illness forced him to relinquish that task in 1988. Adrian Ryans enthusiastically accepted my invitation to assume these responsibilities as well as the directorship of the Management Training Course. The impact of Adrian's management of executive education would manifest itself dramatically in a very short time in terms of revitalizing our courses, as well as in the establishment of our Executive MBA Program a few years later.

Beyond Canada, teams of Western faculty offered a series of two and three-week Executive Programs in Brazil, beginning in 1975, with the encouragement and support of Jake Moore, then CEO of Brascan and a long-time member of our Advisory Committee. Although I had done the feasibility study and directed the first program, John Nicholson enthusiastically directed and championed these activities in subsequent years until his passing in 1981. A drop in the value of Brazilian currency at this time made it prohibitively expensive to continue this venture.

With funding assistance from the Canadian International Development Agency (CIDA), the School ran a two-week General Management Program in Kenya from 1983 to 1987. Harry Lane served as Director of Western's faculty team for the first two years followed by Dave Burgoyne and Randy Kudar. Over the period some 170 Kenyan managers attended the program and a number of cases were produced for use back at Western.

In late 1981, CIDA announced a program to fund linkages between eight Chinese universities and eight Canadian business schools to assist China in developing its management capabilities. Western was chosen as one of the Canadian schools to be twinned with a Chinese institution. Further discussions, in 1982, lead to our conclusion that linkage

with the school, as proposed by Ottawa, was not, an appropriate one for Western and we withdrew from the project.

By 1983, however, the relationship between Queen's University and its assigned partner, Tsinghua University in Beijing, was not working out and Tsinghua requested that CIDA approach us regarding our replacing Queen's as their linkage school. Tsinghua was one of the most prestigious universities in China, and is often referred to as China's MIT. Joe DiStefano and I visited Tsinghua in December of that year and returned with a four-year contract covering MBA training at Western for potential Tsinghua faculty members, extended visits of current

Tsinghua faculty, provision of computer equipment, library and teaching materials and some teaching by Western faculty in China.

Joe DiStefano managed this first-phase contract so adroitly that good relationships were firmly established. Later, a second five-year contract was negotiated and managed by Don Simpson, then Director of our Centre for International Business Studies, and subsequently by Paul Beamish. By the end of this contract 10 volumes of Western cases and/or text material would be translated into Chinese and 12 decision-oriented cases and eight journal articles relating to business in China would be completed.

---

## "...you go to a great school not so much for knowledge, as for arts and habits..."

*Bud Johnston in addressing the graduating classes over the years, frequently included the following quote of William Johnson Cary, a 19th century master at Eton:*

*"At school you are not engaged so much in acquiring knowledge as in making mental efforts under criticism. A certain amount of knowledge can, indeed, with average faculties, acquire so as to retain. Nor need you regret the hours you spend on much that is forgotten for the shadow of lost knowledge at least protects you from many illusions.*

*But, you go to a great school not so much for knowledge, as for arts and habits: for the habit of attention; for the art of expression; for the art of assuming, at a moment's notice, a new intellectual*

*position; for the art of entering quickly into another person's thoughts; for the habit of submitting to censure and refutation; for the art of indicating assent or dissent in graduated terms; for the habit of regarding minute points of accuracy; for the art of working out what is possible in a given time for taste, for discrimination and for mental courage."*

---

*"Andrew Grindlay, a long-time faculty member and Business Quarterly author agreed, in Japan, to take on the job of Editor over one of the most expensive meals I ever bought – a fine investment it turned out..."*

The *Business Quarterly* celebrated its 50th year of continuous publication in 1983 at a time when many university publications across North American were falling by the wayside in the face of rising costs. Doreen Sanders, Editor at the time, as she had been since the early 1960s, had done an absolutely outstandingly creative job of managing the magazine, as well as many of the School's other publications, not only from an editorial standpoint but also from a business aspect as well. Among other honors,

she received the Order of Canada in 1987 for her contributions to Canadian publishing and journalism education. Her stepping down in 1988 after 25 years and 100 continuous issues, posed a real challenge in locating a successor. Andrew Grindlay, a long-time faculty member, and regular *Business Quarterly* author, who was on sabbatical at the time, agreed to take on the job after our meeting in Japan over one of the most expensive meals I had ever bought – a fine investment it turned out as Andrew has done a superb job of continuing and enhancing the *Quarterly* tradition as Canada's unique management journal.

A capable and committed administrative and support staff had for many years been a key factor in the School's success. In earlier years, people such as Margaret Park, Angela Challenor, Pat Avery and Ann Carden had set the standard for service to students, faculty and the business community alike. These traditions were continued strongly and developed further by Lynne Lesko (now Sheridan), Daphne

Stevens and Ella Strong in our student services and program management offices and by their counterparts managing our case and publications office, our library, our print shop, our AV/TV facility and other aspects of our operations. Nancy Graham, with wide-ranging, staff-management responsibilities, played a key role in moving the School forward on a number of important dimensions. John Irwin, our Director of Financial Resources, kept us critically aware as budgets tightened.

Personally, I had enjoyed outstanding support particularly from my assistants Jean Robertson for 15 of the early years, and from Bev Lennox during my first 10 years as Dean, before she moved on to manage, very capably, our office of executive education.

In the spring of 1989, I concluded with regret that in view of my health, it would be inappropriate to continue as Dean. I was confident the School was in a strong position to address the changing roles of business education as we approached the 21st century.

Throughout my 35 years of association with the School as student, teacher, administrator and dean, I had the outstanding opportunity to work with many, varied and talented students, colleagues and members of the business and university communities. I cherish, deeply, the many lifelong friendships I established as we worked together to build the institution and its impact on the practice of management throughout Canada and beyond. The mission of the Western Business School had been, and would continue to be, a noble one as we came more and more to appreciate the central role of management in the development of all aspects of global society. Successors would go on to further fulfill that mission and, in doing so, extend Western's performance and reputation as one of the world's centres of excellence for management education.

"If you couldn't teach, you couldn't stay."

# From slide-rule to lap-top in 30 years

*Alexander (Al) Mikalachki has been a 30-year contributor to the School's preeminence as a teacher, researcher, administrator and Acting Dean (1989-1990). He was the first Ph.D. graduate in Business Administration at Western (1964) as well as the first in Canada. He recounts how, in this chapter written in 1992, during his time, the most dramatic changes have taken place in the classroom and are demographic, attitudinal and technological.*

I remember, in 1960, Western had a stranglehold on degree programs in business administration. The HBA Program held a strong competitive position and the MBA Program was the only one offered in Canada. Selection into both programs was based on leadership qualities and academic grades. The MBA Program also took into account work experience. Today, not much has changed in selection criteria except that the MBA Program uses GMAT (a graduate record exam) scores as an added criterion for admission.

During the late sixties a gradual increase in competitive business programs emerged. In time, over 30 schools offered MBA Programs and significantly more than that offered undergraduate business programs. Recruitment and program content took on new importance in attracting students. Western had to engage in national and international recruitment to attract the best applicants to their programs. The continual updating of course content provided a competitive advantage for recruiting. Since current cases reflect the management issues of the day, our case teaching kept us at the forefront of knowledge.

The most dramatic changes, in the last 30 years, took place in the classroom. The changes were demographic, attitudinal, and technological. Today the classrooms include women, are more egalitarian, and use high technology.

From 1933 to 1972, 72 women had received an H.B.A. degree and 12 an M.B.A. degree from Western. Often, these women would be the only woman in the class. It was not until 1973 that women, 13 of them, were among the graduates in significant numbers: 5, along with 187 of their male classmates, received M.B.A. degrees and 8 accompanied by 105 males, were on hand to receive B.A. degrees in Honors Business.

Because of industry's long antipathy, few women thought about careers in business and it was not until the early 1960s that leading business schools opened their classrooms to women. Harvard Business School did not accept women into its two-year MBA Program until the fall of 1963. It was 1958 when the first woman, Jan Heuber, received her M.B.A. degree from Western.

J.J. Wettlaufer, who at the time was Dean of the School, spoke at the graduating ceremonies and rightly predicted, "there will be a dramatic increase of women into the world of management and it will be welcomed. The complexities of a rapidly changing world needs the best qualities of both men and women. The differences in the sexes will provide a new,

**Joining the ranks of business management were these nine women, who, in 1973, were in the graduating classes at Western Business School. They were nine of the 13 who received either an M.B.A. or B.A. Honors Business degree. (From left to right) Olga Volkoff, M.B.A.; Tevya Rosenberg, H.B.A.; Catherine Gray, M.B.A.; Joan Bennett, M.B.A.; Shelley Brunton, H.B.A.; Patricia Buchanan, H.B.A.; Rose Ho, H.B.A.; Sherry Bowyer, M.B.A.; and Danielle Carle, M.B.A.**

exciting and enriching contribution to the field of management in the future."

By 1990, the MBA class averaged 25% women members and the HBA class averaged 30% women. Six percent of the full-time faculty were women, and it is likely that HBAs and MBAs experienced at least one woman professor in their two years of course work at the Business School.

The place of women in management is still evolving. However, it does not take a clairvoyant to see that their place will be one of equality and effectiveness, the same status that they have held in our programs over the last 25 years.

Classroom attitudes towards formality have changed considerably over the years. In the early twenties, students and faculty wore gowns, in the sixties, students and faculty wore shirts and ties and referred to each other as Professor, Sir or Mister. First names, jeans and T-shirts were not in vogue. Changes in attitude and attire resulted from a cultural revolution in which ideas gained power over position: what was said became more important than who said it. In addition, those who carried out decisions or were affected by them wanted to be part of the decision-making process. Thus, the relationship between boss and subordinate, professor and student shifted from power relations to collaborative undertakings. Criticism and judgment were not suspended - they actually increased. However, they now came from both sides. Professors evaluated students, who in turn evaluated professors.

During this change in which ideas came to prevail over position, there was considerable overt and oblique resistance. They first had to do with the casual or untidy appearance of students who wore T-shirts and jeans to class. There was an equating by some professors of dishevelled clothes and dishevelled minds – the assumption being that sloppy clothes were a forerunner of sloppy minds. This was soon followed by the question, "Are we going to let the inmates run the asylum?" when students questioned some program offerings. Neither of these views reflected much more than resistance to change, however: the juggernaut was in motion and nothing has stopped it – ideas and expertise ruled much of the eighties and early nineties.

The major mechanical device students of the sixties had to deal with was the slide rule: an aid to addition, subtraction and division. Match that with its replacement in the late eighties, a lap-top computer. The age of information has made computer literacy one of the major changes in the MBA Program requirements over the last 30 years. The organization and analysis of seemingly infinite amounts of information has significantly altered schools of management. It has bankrupted their budgets and changed their program content. How it will ultimately unfold is still before us, but we know that where expertise, ideas and information prevail, computer literacy is of paramount importance.

**"Teaching methods have changed. In the early '60s, case discussion in its purest form prevailed...today, more can be presented in an active manner."**

Another major change has been the shift of geographical focus from Canadian markets to world markets. This shift was foreshadowed by the increasing importance of business/government relations. In the seventies, many schools added business/government relations to their programs, recognizing the significant impact that government had on business practices. That government input has now been taken to its natural conclusion - the importance of government when engaging in world markets. Our Free Trade Agreement certainly reflects the inextricable relations among business, government and world markets.

Finally, teaching methods have changed. In the early sixties, case discussion in its purest form prevailed. There was little in the way of non-case readings and less in the way of lectures. Today, as a result of a significant investment in business research world-wide, more is known and more can be presented in a didactic manner. Although the case is still our major teaching tool, present methodologies include videos, lectures, computer simulations, exercises, and a variety of interactional experiences. Of interest, at the moment, are computer hook-ups to the classroom which allow different assumptions, such as changing prices or costs, to be immediately tested for their consequences.

Many changes have taken place in the classroom over 30 years. Our attire and relationships are less formal. Women are very much a part of classroom life. Technological sophistication and a variety of pedagogical approaches are experienced by participants. The development, dissemination and power of ideas prevail.

Although much has changed in terms of means employed, our end or mission is still to improve the practice of management. We pursue this mission, from a teaching point of

"Professor James Taylor, who taught Finance, was probably the most cogent thinker at the School."

view, by developing in our students an ability to define, analyze and solve important unstructured problems. In effect we develop their abilities to define significant problems, determine the root causes, isolate the causes that can be changed directly, and then to develop action plans to resolve the problems. We still aim to develop the problem solvers of the future who will be leaders in our society.

*"The independence I received in the Doctoral Program was both a strength and a weakness."*

Since I was the first Ph.D. graduate in Business Administration at Western (1964), I should share some recollections of that program. For me, the program entailed a year of course work at Western, a year of course work at Cornell University and a year writing my thesis. R.K. Ready, a Western Business School professor, guided the first two years of my program before going on leave to work in Egypt. Dick Hodgson, a newly appointed professor who had just completed his D.B.A. at Harvard, supervised my thesis research.

The independence I received in the program was both a strength and weakness. It allowed me to pursue my own interests and develop a self-reliance. It also had the disquieting features that a lack of structure and tradition entail. Standards of performance were uncertain and comparisons to the one other person in the program were difficult if not impossible. In retrospect, the inner-directedness that the program forced on me and which I readily took to, has served me well in my chosen profession. It is my opinion that above all other capabilities, a professor must be comfortable with independent thought and action. If nothing else, my doctoral experience at Western reinforced my independence of thought.

My thesis defense reflected where business administration stood in the values held by professors of other disciplines at Western. The examination was about four hours in duration and involved professors in the disciplines of Social Science, Natural Science and Arts. Nearly all had come out of a curiosity to witness the singular experience of a student defending a Ph.D. thesis in business administration. Each of the more than 20 professors in attendance posed at least one question. The questions ranged from the place of business in our society and educational system to whether I thought we would have a clean hydrogen bomb. Having no idea of the answer to the latter question, but feeling I had to make a response other than "I don't know," I assumed an expression of studious thought for a moment and answered, "Yes." On this of all days, I wanted to think positively. Incidentally, my thesis was titled: *Group Cohesion Reconsidered*. One professor rather gleefully noted that he had not considered it before, let alone now.

My most satisfying doctoral year was at Cornell, where no one was responsible for me, and thus all the professors were totally encouraging. In one year at Cornell, I took as many courses (Sociology, Social Psychology, Business) as their regular doctoral candidates took in two. I could do so because I did not have to spend time assuaging those in the

system. The course of study and independence offered by my unusual Doctoral Program has served me well as a professor of business administration.

---

*"The School has had an encouraging environment in which students and faculty could grow."*

---

To write about the professors who made an impact at Western is a risky endeavor because of the likelihood that many will be overlooked. Over the years I have learned that students are often profoundly affected by acts or statements by professors who themselves are unaware of the effect of their actions. However, at the risk of overlooking deserving people, I do want to note some professors who have affected the School's programs and life.

Professor Walter Thompson has, over the years, fostered a positive environment in the School. He has probably never met a student he did not like or a person in whom he did not see some good. Walter's positive reinforcement and encouragement have helped many people to reach beyond their grasp and thus become more than they originally thought they could be. His legacy to the School has been a supportive, encouraging environment in which students and faculty could grow.

Professor Jim Taylor, who taught Finance at the School, was probably the most cogent thinker to teach at the School. His ability to simplify the complex was legendary. At times his impulsive impishness had him complicate the simple. However, to engage in a confrontation of logic with Professor Taylor was a losing proposition. Although Jim portrayed a tough exterior, it appeared that this was a mechanism to hide the basic warmth and goodwill he had for others. Both students and faculty became clearer thinkers as a result of exposure to Jim Taylor.

**Dr. Harold Crookell introduced the International Management Course that reflects the inextricable relations among business, government and world markets.**

Professor David Leighton was a major force in developing the Marketing Courses at Western. He was, at one time, the Editor of *Business Quarterly*. He also enhanced relations between the business world and the School, a strength we have continued to develop.

A number of professors have been particularly creative in developing new course offerings. Professor Don Thain has led the way in many new courses, the most notable of which are Business and Society, a revamping of Business Policy, and Business and Government. Professor Dick Hodgson is a most creative designer of courses. Among courses he has developed are: Career Management, Creative Professional Leadership, and Sustainable Growth.

Professors David Kuechle and David Peach, both at other universities now, will be remembered for developing high student interest in Personnel Administration and Labor Relations. In general, the faculty as a whole should take a bow for keeping courses current through the case-writing and consulting activities which keep them abreast of managerial issues.

Over the years there has been a significant growth in our Executive Education Programs (formerly called Continuing Education Programs). Our growth built on two highly successful courses, the Management Training Course (MTC) directed by Walter Thompson and the Marketing Management Course (MMC) directed by Jack Wettlaufer. Professors Bud Johnston and Dave Burgoyne were instrumental in expanding our course offerings. The first wave of expansion included the addition of other functional courses: Production/ Operations Management Course (POMC) directed by Professor Bert Wood, Management for Accounting and Financial Executives (MACFE) directed by Professor Ross Archibald, and the International Management Course (IMC) directed by the late Professor Harold Crookell. The next wave was to provide more advanced, senior courses that dealt with more strategic issues. Two courses were added: the Senior Executives' Program (SEP) directed

by Professor Nick Fry and the Executive Marketing Program for technology-based businesses (EMP) directed by Professor Adrian Ryans. The primary purpose of these new programs was to respond to the growing demand for educating executives to cope in an increasingly competitive and changing environment. Secondarily, but of significant importance, the programs generated much needed funds to operate the School.

---

*"In the '90s we know it is imperative to make the manager's perspective a global one."*

---

The late eighties found the School's faculty and staff working hard at developing a strategy for the next decade. Stimulated by changing environmental conditions and prodded by the School's Advisory Committee, the faculty committed countless hours to developing a strategy. The results were gratifying and received the support of faculty, staff and advisors.

As a school we continue our mission of improving the practice of management. However, we know it is imperative to make the manager's perspective a global one. In effect, we are developing managers to deal with global competition. To do so requires the writing of global cases and the developing of courses to reflect cultural differences as well as global issues. We have also expanded our student exchange to include more countries, and to support faculty exchanges in which we receive foreign faculty and send some of our own

faculty members abroad. We realize that it will take time and investment to globalize our programs. It will also take learning – what skills and knowledge does a global manager require? Our case approach has been instrumental in helping us learn about global management. Our end goal is not to simply add a few courses, but rather to globalize the perspective of our programs, students, staff and faculty.

Research has also taken a prominent position in our strategy. Although teaching is our distinctive competence, without research it would be difficult to attract new faculty to the School and equally difficult to keep current faculty mentally adroit and enthusiastically involved in their teaching responsibilities. We have added to our faculty in order to fulfill our commitment to research.

Financially our new strategy (globalization and research) could not have come at a worse time. University budgets are shrinking, and the economy is flattening out and contracting. Funding needs for case-writing, program development, research expansion and new facilities have risen at an unprecedented level for our School.

We are fortunate to have managed our financial reserves well. Support from Canadian corporations through the Plan for Excellence campaign, from students through alumni donations and from our own executive education surpluses have allowed us to contemplate growth when all other faculties are retrenching their goals. However, to achieve our long-term strategy requires more funds than are available.

Thus a key role of the dean's office continues to be that of fund-raising. A plan has been developed to increase contributions from our key sources: students, Canadian companies, and executive education. Executive education is to be the source of at least half of our external funding needs. It is imperative that we show alumni and corporations that we can earn a great deal of the money we need. By expanding our Executive Education Programs and embarking on an Executive MBA Program we are confident that our goals can be achieved. We also are comfortable in the alumni fund-raising programs we developed, which in time will grow an endowment that will generate substantial annual surpluses. Our Case and Publications Program has also developed into a major funds generator.

The one questionable source of funds is grants from Canadian corporations. Much has changed in the corporate funding environment. Other schools are seeking funds, profits are down, and corporate giving committees are in place. In effect, there is less money to go around, more people after it and it is more difficult (costly) to reach the donors. This corporate giving branch of our fund-raising plan is still a problem in search of a solution. In all probability the School will have to rely much more on alumni giving and executive education profits for future external funding.

---

## "Fortunately, we had a strategy and an effective management team."

---

Through a set of unforeseen circumstances, I took on the role of Acting Dean for the 1989-1990 year. Samual Johnson once said, "When a man knows he is to be hanged, it concentrates his mind wonderfully." Becoming the dean has much the same result. Within two minutes of stepping into the office, I received a phone call from an alumni congratulating me on my

appointment and asking me to intervene on behalf of a young man who was having difficulty entering the MBA Program. The remainder of my year's tenure was a repetition of this initial welcome: either someone came to me or I went to someone else seeking support. A series of problems demanded decisions, some to be made immediately, and fortunately, a few which allowed due time.

Fortunately, we had a strategy and an effective management team (program and administrative directors). Each major decision was evaluated in terms of how it enhanced the strategy and how we could get implementors to buy into the decision. The more difficult and time-consuming decisions were those that were resisted by the implementors but vital to our strategy. These circumstances required discussion and modification so that we both advanced our strategy and had highly motivated implementors. The latter is important in all organizations but more so among academics, each of whom believes that he/she is the CEO.

During my year in the dean's office, the role and power of our administrative staff (mostly women) and gender equity in the School became issues. As a school, we moved forward on both issues. Administrators were given more responsibility and the effective manner in which they managed it gave them more power. As for gender equity, we came to realize the dominance of men, particularly in our faculty. An exploratory study of gender equity in the programs and the School was initiated by Terry Deutscher (Associate Dean, Human Resources). The study generally reported that gender equity prevailed in the School and its programs. However, some needs for significant improvement were noted. It will take many years before the School has a healthy

balance of women faculty members. In 1991, 6% of full-time faculty were women. However, the need for improvement is recognized and plans to do so are evolving.

---

## "The past is prologue to the future."

---

The past is prologue to the future. As of 1990, the School has achieved its earlier goals. The Degree Programs and Executive Education Programs are serving Canadian managers well. A 1987 national study of CEOs, students and deans ranked the Western Business School as number one in the country by each of these groups. The Case and Publications Program is generating material for education purposes second only to Harvard's program. Research is taking on a new importance and should bear fruit in the next decade. Although funding is constrained, the School has sufficient reserves for the next couple of years to allow it to plan and carry out new initiatives.

Those involved in the School's history should take pride in its achievements. The School's prominence in Canada is beyond anyone's early expectations. The future is challenging, but the School will persevere and progress as it has in the past. Excellent students, faculty and staff will continue to overcome obstacles and develop successful, viable programs.

# Becoming world-class

*For the past decade, Adrian Ryans has had a distinguished association with the School as teacher, researcher, administrator and Dean (1990- ). As visionary leader, he has met the challenge of establishing the School as one of the leading centres for management development in the world. This has been in response to the international competition in the global business education market. In this chapter, written in 1993, he discusses how this task was accomplished and also sets out some of the incredible challenges the School now faces and why he is confident it will achieve new heights of excellence in the 21st century as it enhances its reputation as one of the world's leading centres for management development.*

I was in Santa Cruz, California when Terry Deutscher, the School's Associate Dean – Human Resources, called to tell me that Bud Johnston was resigning the deanship due to his deteriorating health, and that Al Mikalachki was going to be Acting Dean, while the University undertook its search for a new dean. It did not occur to me at all on that June, 1989 day that I would become the next dean of the Western Business School.

Prior to 1988, I had had no administrative responsibilities in the School. In 1987, a team of four Marketing faculty members, Terry Deutscher, Ken Hardy, Roger More and I, had proposed to the Director of Continuing Education, Dave Burgoyne, that we launch a new marketing program for executives in technology-based businesses. From the very beginning we wanted this program to be a world-class program targeted at the North American and even the global market. We felt that we could offer a world-class experience and should charge a world-class price for the program. There was some skepticism in the School that executives would pay Harvard or Stanford prices to attend a program in London, Ontario, Canada. However, we were successful in convincing our colleagues that this was feasible. We agreed that I would be the team leader for this program, and we successfully launched the Executive Marketing Program for technology-based businesses in February, 1988.

Later that year, with a deterioration in the health of Dave Burgoyne, the Director of Continuing Education, Bud Johnston asked me if I would succeed Dave. I agreed to do this. At that time, Bud was still the Director of the Management Training Course, Canada's first, and Western's largest and most profitable executive program. Given his responsibilities as

Dean, he had not had a lot of time to devote to program strategy in the preceding years. We agreed that I would be Co-Director of the Management Training Course in 1988 and would take over the directorship in 1989 with the view to working with the faculty to undertake a major restructuring of the program. I asked three of the faculty working on the program, Nick Fry, Jeff Gandz and Larry Wynant to work with me to undertake this restructuring. Although I had never worked closely with these individuals before, it turned out to be a great team. After conducting market research with alumni and others, and some highly productive meetings, we agreed to a radical restructuring of the program. We decided to shorten the program by a week, change its location to Spencer Hall from Medway, radically restructure the content and organization, offer it twice a year instead of once a year, and increase the weekly price by almost 50%. We relaunched the Management Training Course as the Western Executive Program in the spring of 1989 and its success exceeded our expectations. Until the recession of the early 1990s began to bite in 1991, one of my biggest challenges as Program Director, was turning away qualified applicants, who we simply couldn't accommodate in the program. These two executive education experiences, the creation of the Executive Marketing Program and the relaunching of the Western Executive Program, were to me among the most satisfying experiences of my professional life. It was great to see what small teams of talented faculty and staff could accomplish when they put their minds to a task.

I assume that these successes which I contributed to in executive education were major reasons for the Dean's Selection Committee offering me the position of Dean in June, 1990. I had initially indicated to the committee that I had no interest in such an administrative job but when other potential candidates were eliminated by the committee,

"We felt we could offer a world-class experience and charge a world-class price for the programs."

Tom Collins, the Provost of the University, asked me to reconsider.

My family, while not enthusiastic, was supportive of me taking the position. My mother, who was 85 and terminally ill in the summer of 1990, was quite excited, when I accepted the position. When my father had died in 1960, I had persuaded my mother to pick up her roots and move to Canada, which I viewed as a 'land of opportunity'. This courageous woman, who had never worked in her married life and had no job qualifications,

packed up all her belongings and emigrated to Canada with a 15 year-old son and a 12 year-old daughter and less than $5,000 in her pocket. To her, some of my professional successes had made her sacrifices worthwhile.

Before assuming the deanship in September, 1990, I spent time talking to a variety of faculty and staff in the Business School and to some knowledgeable outsiders, such as Dick Currie, the President of Loblaws and the Chair of the Business School's Advisory Committee. As a result of this process, I concluded that there were a number of major issues facing the Business School. It was very clear that one of these issues was the rapid globalization of the business education market. The Western Business School had been very active internationally for many years, having undertaken major initiatives in the West Indies, Kenya, and the Peoples Republic of China. Many of our older faculty had spent a year teaching at such European schools as IMEDE[1] (now IMD) in Switzerland and INSEAD[2] in France. We were one of the first schools in North America to launch an exchange program, when we linked up with the London Business School in the United Kingdom in 1976. While superficially we were quite international, our orientation was still fundamentally that of a Canadian school. When we thought about competition (which we didn't do very often!) we worried about other Canadian business schools. However, it was very apparent in the late 1980s in our MBA acceptance data that our competition was increasingly international. In the mid-1980s, when we lost a potential student to another business school, that school was almost invariably another Canadian school, such as Queen's, McGill, or the University of Toronto. By 1990, this had changed radically. Now, when we lost an applicant to another school, that school was much more likely to be a U.S. or European school. The situation was similar in faculty recruiting. We were by then clearly competing for faculty with leading business schools from all over the world, including those in Europe and Asia.

**The graduating HBA Class of '92 reflected the School's determination to position itself as a competitor in the global business education market.**

*"I felt that we needed to fundamentally restructure our thinking and view ourselves as a school challenging itself to become widely regarded as one of the leading centres for management development in the world."*

There were also some advantages to us thinking of ourselves as a competitor in the global business education market. My experiences in executive education had convinced me that we had become frozen in our attitudes. Our perspective was very much that of the premier business school in Canada defending its leadership position. I felt that we needed to fundamentally restructure our thinking and view ourselves as a school challenging itself to become widely regarded as one of the leading centres for management development in the world. An orientation towards attack rather than defence was fundamentally much more appealing to me. The environment in 1990 seemed like a perfect opportunity to make the change. Our successes in launching the Executive Marketing Program and radically restructuring the Western Executive Program had given many of the faculty and staff the confidence that we could make quite radical changes in strategy and be very successful. I also felt that if we didn't start making some

---

[1] IMEDE   Institut pour l'Étude des Methodes de Direction de l'Entreprise
[2] INSEAD   European Institute of Business Administration, now, International Institute for Management Development IMD.

significant changes in the School and its programs, we would lose some of the most creative and productive faculty.

It has also become clear that in the summer of 1990 that we were going to face some very significant budget cuts at The University of Western Ontario. In my two meetings with the Provost, Tom Collins, before accepting the deanship, my main focus had been on trying to negotiate some continued financial independence for the Business School. In particular, I felt that we had to continue to have the right to retain the bulk of our executive education profits within the Business School. Only with access to these kinds of financial resources, could we hope to be competitive on the global scene. Shortly after I became Dean, the University announced a 13.5% budget cut over the next three years. This announcement brought a sense of crisis to the University, and in the Business School. We recognized that fundamental change was going to be necessary. It was about this time that Terry Deutscher, the Associate Dean - Human Resources, and I decided that we should be very open with faculty, staff, students and alumni about the Business School's financial situation. Al Mikalachki had begun doing this during his year as Acting Dean. Jack Wettlaufer and Bud Johnston had taken a very personal responsibility for raising the funds to support our course development and research activities. With the deteriorating financial situation, both Terry Deutscher and I felt that this rapidly growing burden had to be shared more evenly over the faculty and staff. John Irwin, the School's very effective Director of Financial Resources, helped us to organize the financial data on the School into an intelligible format. Then, we undertook a very conscious campaign, beginning at Homecoming in 1990, to communicate the financial realities of the School's very difficult situation to the Business School community, alumni, corporate community, and parents of our students. This

was not always well received. Some alumni and parents, and even our own faculty and staff, felt it was 'crass' to talk about money at events like Parents' Day or Homecoming. But we persevered, because we felt that we had to communicate to our stakeholders that they could no longer assume that a world-class education would be funded solely by the taxpayers.

---

*"Giving the women managers and staff a greater leadership role seemed a very good way to reduce some of the gender inequities that were perceived to exist in the School."*

---

In addition to the financial resources that we would need to pursue the vision of becoming widely recognized as a world-class centre for management development, we would also need the human resources. We were clearly going to need more leadership, creativity and hard work, if we were going to undertake a large number of new initiatives. Also, as the business education market became more competitive, the quality and professionalism of everything we did would have to increase dramatically. It seemed to many of the faculty in leadership roles in the School that we would have to place increasing reliance on our staff, if we were to succeed. We have always been very fortunate at the Western Business School to have many highly effective individuals on our support staff. But, I felt that we could no longer just view them as 'support staff'. I had seen this in my two years in executive education, where much of what we had accomplished there had been the result of the creative ideas and initiative of individuals like Beverly Lennox, Sheryl Gregson and Marilyn Senft. We would need to unleash talented staff in all areas of the

School and have them play a more active role in the development and implementation of strategies in their particular areas. This was reinforced by the preliminary findings of the Gender Equity Committee that had been established by Al Mikalachki in 1989. The leadership of the School was male-dominated and this didn't always create a 'friendly' environment for the female managers and staff. Giving the women managers and staff in the School a greater leadership role seemed to me a very good way to reduce some of the gender inequities that were perceived to exist in the School.

One of my first actions as dean was to initiate steps to put the Western Business School on a firmer financial footing. This involved putting a higher priority on some of the executive education initiatives I had been involved in over the previous two years. The second major initiative was to give a much higher priority to corporate and alumni development within the School.

---

*"A major decision that Peter Killing and I faced in the fall of 1990 was the location of some space in Mississauga that could be converted into a world-class executive development centre for the EMBA Program."*

---

When I took over as dean, the planning for the Executive MBA initiative was well underway. As Director of Executive Education, I had been successful in working with our faculty and the University administration to get approval for the program. Peter Killing had agreed to be the Founding Director of the program for a three-year term beginning in the summer of 1990. A major decision that Peter and I faced in the fall of 1990 was the location of some space in Mississauga that could be converted into a world-class executive development centre for

**Peter Killing in the classroom.**

1991 to work with a developer to build a facility near the Delta Meadowvale hotel in Mississauga. The contract was signed in late February, 1991, with a deadline to have a building designed and opened by September of that year in order to be ready for the entering EMBA class. I know that Peter Killing and I both spent some sleepless nights over this decision. Here we were committing about $2 million of the School's resources to the building of a classroom facility in Mississauga, when we didn't even have one student definitely signed up for the Executive MBA Program. As a result of a tremendous effort by Nancy Graham, our Project Manager, and Dennis LeMay from the University's Physical Plant Department, the facility was opened, on time, in September, 1991.

In signing a 15-year lease for the facility, we had written into the contract the option to purchase the facility from the developer at a prearranged price at specified times during the lease period. As part of the University's Renaissance Campaign, the Western Business School had raised about $2 million for a third floor addition to the National Centre for Management Research and Development. The need for this additional space had been identified in the late 1980s when the School was undergoing a heady phase of growth in faculty and staff. With the realities of budget cutting and down-sizing of the early 1990s, it was rapidly becoming clear that additional space was not a high priority. Terry Deutscher and I felt that a much better use for these resources might be the purchase of the Executive Development Centre in Mississauga. This view was supported strongly by Dick Currie, who felt that we should own, not lease, land and buildings, a position he had championed at Loblaws. The lead donor for the third floor expansion of the NCMRD was the

the EMBA Program. While we had initially looked at purchasing a facility, we had dismissed this option due to the high cost of purchasing the land and constructing the facility. Peter looked at a number of potential facilities that could be leased in the fall of 1990, but was unable to identify one that really met our needs. As the recession began to hit, real estate prices and construction costs started to plummet in Mississauga and we decided to take another look at the option of having a facility constructed to our specifications and leased on a long-term basis. At that time Peter Killing lived next door to me in London and there were a couple of weekends where we traded spreadsheets back an forth as we tried to decide on the viability of building our own facility. After discussions with several members of the faculty and staff and Dick Currie, Chair of the Advisory Committee, we decided in early

**"In my first two years in the position, Terry Deutscher (centre) was effectively Co-Dean."**

Ivey family. We approached the Iveys in the spring of 1992 to determine whether they would be willing to transfer their funding from the NCMRD to the Executive Development Centre in Mississauga. Dick and Beryl Ivey, and their son Richard and daughter Rosamond, all of whom are graduates of Western, (three of the Western Business School) met Peter Killing and me one Friday in Mississauga to view the facility and to discuss the Executive MBA Program. By the end of the meeting, the family was very excited about redirecting their donation to the Mississauga facility. We had indicated we would be willing to name the facility after the Ivey family. But in a telephone conversation about a week later, Dick Ivey very generously suggested that the family would be delighted if the facility were to be named in honor of J.J. Wettlaufer. Both the Wettlaufer family and the Business School community were delighted with this idea. Having Jack's name attached to the Executive Development Centre made it very easy for us to persuade the other donors to the third floor addition to redirect their gifts to Mississauga as well. The purchase was consummated in early 1993.

Also in the fall of 1990, we had been heavily involved in the University's decision to expand Spencer Hall, the executive development facility in London that was jointly operated by The Bank of Nova Scotia and The University of Western Ontario. With the growth of executive education at the Business School, we could no longer book enough space in the original Spencer Hall facility to meet our needs. Therefore, the University and the Bank agreed to double the size of this facility to meet the needs of both the Business School and other University and corporate users. This $8 million expansion was designed to create a world-class residential executive development centre that would be able to meet the needs of the Western Business School and the other users in the years to come. We were actively involved in the

**Spencer Hall, the executive development facility jointly operated by the Bank of Nova Scotia and The University of Western Ontario since 1978, was doubled in size in 1992 to meet the needs of both the Western Business School and corporate users.**

design of the addition. Beverley Lennox played the key role in this regard as she very ably represented the Business School on the Spencer Hall Planning Committee.

During the period 1990 to 1993, we also saw a rapid expansion of our custom programs business. These programs were not only beneficial from a financial viewpoint, but also contributed to keeping our faculty up-to-date with current issues facing leading-edge businesses.

Another early priority was corporate and alumni development. Early in the fall of 1990, Terry Deutscher and I agreed that we should put much greater emphasis on this area. To provide greater staff capability in the alumni development area, I approached Lynne Sheridan, who was at that time, Director of Student Services. Lynne had been very successful in developing the team of Larysa Gamula, Ella Strong and Daphne Stevens to run Admissions, Programs and Career Services respectively. With this team functioning very well, Lynne had a much more limited role and was looking for new challenges. We were

convinced that she would have the energy and enthusiasm to really stimulate the whole alumni development area. We also felt that moving one of our most senior staff members into this area would give the whole alumni development area more credibility and visibility within the School. At about the same time we recruited Terry Pursell to bring more focus to the corporate development area. Over the next two years we saw a number of new initiatives launched in both of these areas, which promise very high, long-run payoffs for the School.

In my first two years in the position, Terry Deutscher was effectively Co-Dean. Having served as Associate Dean for three-and-one-half years, he had an excellent understanding of all of the issues facing the School, and I made no significant decisions without his input. Terry has that rare ability to be able to see to the core of any issue and can always generate a series of creative alternatives. Al Mikalachki, who was in the process of returning to full-time teaching,

# 20 Leading business schools offering the executive MBA. *(Reprinted from Business Week)*

For years, business-school deans talked about putting more international content into U.S. classrooms. Now, many of them are taking the notion a bit further – sending their executive MBA students overseas. Nearly half of the nation's executive MBA programs boast study tours abroad, up from just 25% five years ago.

All the schools on *Business's Week* list of executive MBA leaders offer an international seminar or study tour with the exception of Columbia University and the University of Washington. Columbia University's program will begin offering an international seminar next year. Some schools make the trips mandatory, while others offer them as pricey options.

But a growing number of schools are serving up more than just a single overseas adventure. In addition to a one-week trip to Japan, Washington University's Olin School provides a four-week elective on finance and capital markets in London. EMBAs at the University of Texas can study in England, Mexico, and France.

While critics belittle some of these trips as little more than group vacations, more schools than ever are making them demanding educational whirlwinds. UCLA uses its international trip as a key component of a six-month-long consulting project for a non-U.S. company. This year EMBAs are studying Nokia, a Finnish telecommunications company. New York University

requires executives to study Japanese or Russian economics and history before exporting them to Japan or the former Soviet Union for a week-long residency tied directly to courses on global strategy and general managers.

Back at home, the programs don't differ all that much. They offer seminar-style MBAs for managers with a decade or more of work experience. The programs tend to run for two years, and classes usually meet on alternating Fridays and Saturdays. Many also require periods of on-campus residency. Students are generally sponsored by their companies, which help foot tuition bills and allow for time off from work to attend class.

| School | Total tuition | Avg. years in work force | Avg. salary of manager | Female enrollment | Highlights |
|---|---|---|---|---|---|
| **Boston,** Tyngsboro, Mass. | $39,825 | 13 | $72,000 | 24% | MBAs select week-long seminar abroad. Traveled to Prague and Budapest last year to study emerging capitalist economies. |
| **Chicago,** Chicago | 42,000 | 15 | 86,000 | 22 | Pioneer of EMBA format is moving program into a new $44 million building next year. Launching program in Barcelona. |
| **Columbia,** New York | 62,500 | 10 | 105,000* | 25 | New curriculum emphasizing four key themes; global management, ethics, quality, and human resources. Will add international project trip. |
| **Duke** (Fuqua), Durham, N.C. | 44,000 | 12 | 88,000* | 12 | Going global by putting more non -U.S. content in core courses, offering international electives. Big users include AT&T IBM, and GE. |
| **Emory,** Atlanta | 39,200 | 15 | 83,000 | 26 | New focus on global marketing and managing customer relationships. Boasts field projects linked to work back at the office. |
| **Illinois,** Urbana-Champaign | 26,200 | 14 | 59,000 | 20 | Putting candidates' companies' cases into classes. Requires consulting project with social-service agencies. Global trip optional. |
| **Michigan State** (Broad), East Lansing | 24,400 | 13 | 60,000 | 12 | Location is prime for big three: GM, Ford, and Chrysler. Now requires 14-day international excursion to Far East or Europe. |
| **Minnesota** (Carlson), Minneapolis | 32,000 | 16 | 65,000* | 25 | Overseas trip to Budapest features course as well as government and company visits. Major clients include 3M, Honeywell, US West, Cargill. |
| **North Western** (Kellogg), Evanston, Ill. | 43,500 | 15 | 99,000 | 19 | Added core course in negotiation and elective in information management. Major clients include GE, Baxter. Foreign trip optional. |
| **NYU** (Stern), New York | 63,200 | 11 | 85,000 | 31 | Attempts to put only star teachers before EMBAs. Half of class travels to Japan, half to Eastern Europe and Russia. |
| **Pennsylvania** (Wharton), Philadelphia | 63,450 | 10 | 109,000 | 31 | Allows exceptional latitude, with students picking 9 of 19 courses. Will launch new and innovative curriculum for EMBAs next year. |
| **Pittsburgh** (Katz), Pittsburgh | 28,000 | 14 | 55,000 | 30 | Added global course and exercises in leadership, communication, and teams. Also offers Purdue-like "Flex" program ideal for out-of-towners. |
| **Purdue** (Krannert), West Lafayette, Ind. | 28,500 | 12 | 94,000 | 22 | Learning via computer: Execs meet only six times, for two-week residencies. Otherwise, they network and study using computers. |
| **Southern California,** Los Angeles | 32,520 | 16 | 79,000 | 29 | Launched strategy consulting project with top managers of client companies. Added six electives, from Great Books to Market Research. |
| **Southern Methodist** (Cox), Dallas | 29,940 | 18 | 92,000 | 20 | Assesses managers, leadership qualities prior to entering program and again at end. Draws experienced crowd, averaging 38 years old. |
| **Texas,** Austin | 21,800 | 12 | 80,000* | 25 | Nearly one in four executives from nonprofit sector. All spend week of program in London. Option to study in Mexico and France. |
| **UCLA** (Anderson), Los Angeles | 44,000 | 14 | 110,000 | 28 | Gone high-tech with "wired" classrooms and laptops. Boosts field-study projects with non-US. companies such as Sony and SGS-Thomson. |
| **Washington,** Seattle | 32,000 | 14 | 60,000 | 40 | Mentor program matches entering managers with EMBA alumni to help them adjust to demands of balancing full-time job with school. |
| **Washington (Olin),** St. Louis | 39,3000 | 14 | 65,000 | 26 | Washington, D.C., and Tokyo residencies. Students also spend four weeks in London for credit as part of summer elective option. |
| **Western Ontario,** London, Ont. | 31,580 | 14 | 70,000* | 18 | One of Canada's best B-schools launched program in 1991. Boasts "best-practices forum" to aid in benchmarking, and study in China. |

*Business Week estimate

served as Associate Dean, Programs, for the first year of my deanship. Al could always be counted on for sage advice. But, perhaps one of the major accomplishments of the early 1990s was the identification of several individuals who were able to provide leadership for a number of initiatives and programs within the School. Without a doubt, Peter Killing did a tremendous job of converting a paper Executive MBA Program into a real Executive MBA Program that was already, by the fall of 1993, being included in *Business Week's* list of the top 20 executive MBA programs in the world. I was even more delighted when, in the spring of 1992, Peter agreed to take over as one of the Associate Deans with particular responsibility for executive education. Claude Lanfranconi, who replaced me as Director of the Western Executive Program in the fall of 1990, was another inspired choice. Claude turned out to be highly effective, both at dealing with the faculty team and with participants. He showed a tremendous commitment of time and energy to further improving this key program for the School. When Paul Beamish indicated that he wanted to give up the directorship of the Centre for International Business Studies, so that he could devote more of his energy to the *Journal of International Business Studies*, I asked him to develop a list of potential successors. I did the same. I think we were both surprised when John Kennedy's name appeared on the top of both of our lists. John agreed to take over the position and in a very short time was bringing leadership and energy to this quite time-consuming position within the School. When Jim Rush, Ken Hardy and Christoph Haehling von Lanzenauer completed their terms, Jeff Gandz, Kathy Slaughter and Rod White, turned out to be equally competent leaders for our three degree programs, as all these programs faced periods of significant challenge and change. Many other individuals agreed to take on a variety of other major and minor leadership roles within the School. When Terry Deutscher stepped down as Associate Dean of

'everything' in the summer of 1992, Larry Wynant and Peter Killing agreed to take over as Associate Deans with responsibilities for all the faculty and all programs, except for Research and Development, which had been consolidated in 1991 under the very effective management of Jim Hatch when David Leighton stepped down as Director of the NCMRD. Larry Wynant, who had previously served as MBA Program Director, was known as a very hard-working and highly effective leader with an intimate knowledge of the School's degree programs. He proved to be even more effective as Associate Dean. Larry was always willing to take on the tough issues and deal with them in a direct and effective manner. Jim Hatch's six-year term as Research Director and then Associate Dean, Research and Development, came to an end in the summer of 1993 when Jim returned to full-time teaching. We were all sorry to lose Jim's administrative skills. In consolidating the administration of the School's research organization with that of the NCMRD he had faced a number of challenging personnel issues. Throughout this difficult period Jim retained his positive, cheerful attitude and dealt with each of the issues firmly, but sensitively. Ken Hardy agreed to succeed Jim. With his broad experience in the School and his capacity for hard work, I had no doubt that Ken would be a fitting successor to Jim Hatch.

---

*"As a school, we try to make a major attempt to get selected staff more directly involved in the School's decision-making... They played a key role in implementing the decisions that were made."*

---

But, perhaps one of the things of which I am most proud, was the way a number of the School staff continued to grow and make very significant contributions to the School during

the early years of my tenure. As a school, we try to provide selected staff with more educational opportunities and also make a major attempt to get them much more directly involved in the School's decision-making. This was not always welcomed by all members of the faculty, some of whom felt that decision-making in the School should be, largely, a faculty role. Both Terry Deutscher and I disagreed strongly with this attitude. We felt that it was essential to get the staff involved in strategic planning and decision-making for the School. They often had first-hand access to information that faculty were not aware of and they played an absolutely key role in implementing the decisions that were made.

Almost everybody at the School felt that there was a major gap between the perception and the reality of the Western Business School. Particularly, when one traveled outside Canada, few business leaders had heard of the Western Business School. In fact, The University of Western Ontario itself sounded like a second or third-tier university. Partly to overcome this, we decided to promote the Western Business School as a brand name in its own right and to place less emphasize on the relationship with The University of Western Ontario. To close the gap between the reality and the perception we decided to communicate more pro-actively with the business press, both in Canada and internationally. Margot Northey agreed to play a lead role in this effort. An early success was a set of very favorable rankings by Canadian CEOs, human resource executives and placement specialists in the April 1993 *Canadian Business*. We were particularly pleased with an article that favorably compared our MBA Program with those of Northwestern and the London Business School. It seemed an appropriate moment to celebrate, since we had been steadily cutting budgets and increasing workloads for almost three years, and yet we were continuing to excel. Peter, Larry and I decided to buy everybody in the School a bottle of champagne and to place it on their desks

**The purchase of the Executive Development Centre in Mississauga was consummated in early 1993. At the request of the Ivey family, it was named in honor of J. J. Wettlaufer (Dean, 1963–1978).**

during the night, so that everybody would be surprised by finding a bottle there when they arrived at work the next morning. We had some momentary doubts about the political correctness of champagne in the 1990s, but decided to risk any backlash, since it was such an important symbol of celebration in Western society. As is true so often in business, the strategy is simple to develop, but the implementation is much more difficult. The LCBO was in the midst of an initiative to reduce inventories and didn't have 150 bottles of any brand of champagne in Southwestern Ontario, and it would take over a week to get that much from the warehouse in Toronto. When it did arrive in London, we successfully smuggled the champagne into the School without anybody seeing it and printed 150

letters without Judy Ellis, my Administrative Assistant knowing (no mean achievement!). Then, Larry Wynant and I, as co-conspirators, met on a Sunday evening and with master-keys in hand, went from office to office in the School putting a letter and a bottle on each desk. It took a lot more time than we had estimated, and, unfortunately the so-called 'master-keys' did not open all the offices in the School. The janitors' 'office' had its own key as did the computer support staff's office and the library. The response from the Business School community the next morning was very positive and it seemed to give everybody's morale a boost.

I was also very enthusiastic, when Andrew Grindlay, the Editor and Publisher of the *Business Quarterly* proposed that he create a new, more modern look for the magazine in 1993. The *Business Quarterly* had become a respected management publication under the 25-year leadership of Doreen Sanders. On her retirement, Andrew Grindlay had taken over this role. In his quiet, unassuming way, Andrew was an extremely powerful salesperson, both for the *Business Quarterly* and for the Western Business School. He proved to be as aggressive in pursuing advertisers as he did in pursuing authors for manuscripts. The *Business Quarterly* contributed a good deal to the School's national image.

On the international front, we had a number of visibility-enhancing successes in the early 1990s. Paul Beamish, with the School's support, aggressively went after the editorship of the *Journal of International Business Studies,* the world's leading academic publication in that field. The publication had never been housed outside of the United States, and it was a real coup for Paul to be selected as the Editor and the Western Business School as its home for a five-year period beginning in 1993.

Both our undergraduate and graduate students had considerable success in case competitions in the United States. In fact, the undergraduates won the University of Virginia's case competition for three years in a row and were asked to withdraw for a couple of years to give other teams a chance! The HBAs own international case competition, created with the strong encouragement of Ken Hardy, gained increasing visibility in the early 1990s as the HBAs brought in teams from all over the world to participate in the tournament at the Western Business School. This created considerable goodwill for the School and a perception of leadership in undergraduate business education. The MBAs were also very active in the international field. Two MBA students, Paul Fitzgerald and Scott Heloffs, were instrumental in launching what became known as the LEADER Project at the Western Business School. This involved a large number of our students going to the Commonwealth of Independent States each summer to conduct management development programs for managers and academics in these emerging market economies. This student-led initiative, with support from External Affairs Canada, provided a powerful educational experience for both the participants and the instructors from our School. In 1993, the MBA students were successful in winning the competition to host the Graduate Business Conference at the Western Business School in 1995. The Graduate Business Conference is an annual conference supported by the Graduate Business Foundation that attracts student leaders from the 35 leading MBA programs in the world to share best practices. It was a real coup for our students, who put together an exciting video about the Western Business School and a very impressive presentation, that resulted in them being selected by the delegates at the 1993 conference over competitive business schools by an overwhelming margin.

As the School enters the last half of the 1990s, it faces some incredible challenges. The global competition for the best students and faculty is reaching new heights, our faculty are aging, and the School faces tremendous financial challenges as it comes into head-to-head competition with Harvard Business School, Wharton, Stanford Business School, INSEAD and other leading global schools. However, I am convinced that with the support of our alumni and the Canadian business community, the faculty, staff and students of the Western Business School will achieve new heights of excellence, and our School will enter the 21st century widely recognized as one of the world's leading centres for management development.

Aerial view of The University of Western Ontario
campus, London, Canada, taken in 1985 during the
construction of the National Centre for Management
Research and Development. The building is part of
Western Business School.

# the
# people
# who
# made it
# happen...

# University of Western Ontario

## Presidents

Bishop Isaac Hellmuth
1878 - 1885

William R. Meredith
1886 - 1900

Walter Hoare Moorhouse
1900 - 1908

Nathaniel Chamney James
1908 - 1914

Edward Ernest Braithwaite
1914 - 1919

Triumverate: (1919 - 1927)
William Sherwood Fox
Paul S. McKibbon
Hibbert W. Hill

William Sherwood Fox
1927 - 1947

George Edward Hall
1947 - 1967

David Carlton Williams
1967 - 1977

George Edward Connell
(8th President of the University)
1977 - 1984

Alan Kenneth Adlington
(9th President of the University: 'numbered' per Board of Governors resolution, although an Acting President)
1984 - 1985 (Acting President)

Knud George Pedersen
(10th President of the University)
1985 - 1994

Paul Theodore Davenport
(11th President of the University)
1994 - 1999 (renewable)

## Chancellors

Rev. Isaac Hellmuth
1878 - 1885

Rev. Alfred Peache
1885 - 1900

Chief Justice Richard Martin Meredith
1909 - 1916

Dr. William James Roche
1916 - 1929

Colonel the Honorable Henry Cockshutt
1929 - 1944

The Honorable George Howard Ferguson
1945 - 1946

Arthur Rutherford Ford
1947 - 1955

Richard Green Ivey
1955 - 1961

Verschoyle Philip Cronyn
1961 - 1967

Albert William Trueman
1967 - 1971

The Honorable John Parmenter Robarts
1972 - 1976

John Allyn Taylor
1976 - 1980

Richard Macaulay Ivey
1980 - 1984

David Black Weldon
1984 - 1988

Grant Louis Reuber
1988 - 1992

Reva Gerstein
1992 - 1996

## Chairs of the Board of Governors

Chief Justice Richard Martin Meredith
1908 - 1914

Charles Ross Somerville
1914 - 1919

Arthur Thomas Little
1919 - 1954

Gordon John Ingram
1955

Douglas Black Weldon
1958 - 1967

Albert Edwin Shepherd
1967 - 1970

Joseph J. Jeffery
1970 - 1973

Richard Macaulay Ivey
1973 - 1976

William C.P. Baldwin
1976 - 1977

Alfred Brandon Conron
1978 - 1980

Geno Frederick Francolini
1980 - 1983

William Alexander Jenkins
1983 - 1985

Robert Gary Siskind
1986 - 1987

Earl H. Orser
1988 - 1989

John S. Brant
1990 - 1991

Claude M.V. Pensa
1991 - 1993

Elizabeth (Libby) Fowler
1994 -

# Western Business School

## Advisory Committee Members 1950 -1993

J.W. Adams, Vice-President Finance, Emco Limited

Alan K. Adlington, Vice-President, Administration and Finance, The University of Western Ontario

John D. Allan, President, The Steel Company of Canada, Limited

J.A. Armstrong, President and Chief Executive Officer, Imperial Oil Limited

Ralph M. Barford, President, General Steel Wares Ltd.

Brig. W.A. Bean, President and General Manager, The Waterloo Trust and Savings Co.

Paul Bienvenu, President, Catelli Food Products

J. Allan Boyle, Executive Vice-President and Chief General Manager, The Toronto-Dominion Bank

John S. Brant, President and Chief Executive Officer, Emco Limited

J.E. Brent, President, International Business Machines Co. Ltd

Thomas H. Brent, President, Brent Surgical Inc.

Robert D. Brown, Vice-Chairman, Price Waterhouse

Claude Bruneau, President, Chairman and Chief Executive Officer, The Imperial Life Assurance Company of Canada

Lt. Col. G. Allan Burton, President, Simpsons Limited

Donald G. Campbell, Chairman and Chief Executive Officer, Maclean-Hunter Ltd.

C. David Clark, President and Chief Executive Officer, Campbell Soup Company Ltd.

Brendan R. Clouston, Executive Vice-President and Chief Operating Officer, Tele-Communications Inc.

George B. Cobbe, President and Chief Executive Officer, Hewlett-Packard (Canada) Ltd.

Dr. George E. Connell, President and Vice-Chancellor, The University of Western Ontario

Dr. A. Brandon Conron, Chairman, The Board of Governors, The University of Western Ontario

E. Jacques Courtois, Q.C., Courtois, Clarkson, Parsons & Tetrault

N.R. Crump, Chairman and Chief Executive Officer, Canadian Pacific

Richard J. Currie, President, Loblaw Companies Ltd.

A. Jean De Grandpre, Chairman and Chief Executive Officer, Bell Canada

H. George De Young, Industrialist

Paul Desmarais, Chairman, Power Corporation of Canada Limited

J.S. Dinnick, President, McLeod, Young, Weir & Co. Ltd.

Professor Joseph J. DiStefano, Associate Dean (Human Resources), School of Business Administration, The University of Western Ontario

Brian P. Drummond, President, Greenshields Inc.

W.L. Duffield, Managing Director, Union Gas Company of Canada Limited, Member, Board of Governors

John C. Eaton, Chairman, Eatons of Canada Ltd.

Rhys T. Eyton, President and Chief Executive Officer, Pacific Western Airlines Ltd.

Robert A. Ferchat, Chairman, Atomic Energy of Canada Limited

F. William Fitzpatrick, President and Chief Executive Officer, Bralorne Resources Limited

Geno F. Francolini, Vice-Chairman and Chief Executive Officer, Livingston Industries Limited

Barbara H. Fraser, Vice-President and General Manager, Paper Products, Procter & Gamble Inc.

J.N. Fry, Associate Professor, Chairman, Research and Publication Program, School of Business Administration, The University of Western Ontario

R. Donald Fullerton, Chairman and Chief Executive Officer, Canadian Imperial Bank of Commerce

Malcolm I.F. Gissing, President and General Manager, Hewlett-Packard (Canada) Ltd.

John F. Graham, Assistant Dean (Administration), School of Business Administration, The University of Western Ontario

Jon K. Grant, President and Chief Executive Officer, The Quaker Oats Company of Canada Ltd.

Donald E. Hackworth, President and General Manager, General Motors of Canada Ltd.

G. Edward Hall, President and Vice-Chancellor, The University of Western Ontario

Margaret L. Hamilton, President and Chief Operating Officer, Thomson Newspapers Limited
Kenneth W. Harrigan, President and Chief Executive Officer, Ford Motor Co. of Canada Ltd.
Russell E. Harrison, Chairman and Chief Executive Officer, Canadian Imperial Bank of Commerce
Eric L. Harvie, Barrister
James E. Hatch, Associate Dean, Western Business School, The University of Western Ontario
W. L. Hawkins, Vice-President and General Manager, Sales Division, Ford Motor Company of Canada Limited
Brig. W.H. Hemphill, President and General Manager, Imperial Furniture Manufacturing Co. Ltd., Member, Board of Governors
J. Claude Herbert, President, Transparent Paper Products Ltd.
D.C. Higginbotham, Price Waterhouse and Company
Wilbert H. Hopper, Chairman and Chief Executive Officer, Petro-Canada
J. William Horsey, Chairman, Salada Foods Ltd.
Richard G. Ivey, Q.C., Barrister
Richard M. Ivey, Q.C., Barrister
Richard W. Ivey, President and Chief Executive Officer, Ivest Corporation
Joseph Jeffery, Q.C., Chairman of the Board of Governors, The University of Western Ontario
Charles B. Johnston, Associate Dean, School of Business Administration, The University of Western Ontario
J. Peter Killing, Associate Dean, Western Business School
Gerald L. Knowlton, President, Knowlton Realty Limited
Calvert C. Knudsen, Chairman and Chief Executive Officer, MacMillan Bloedel Ltd.
Mervyn L. Lahn, President and Chief Executive Officer, The Canada Trust Co.
Allan D. Laird, Chairman, Steel Brothers Canada Ltd.
Allen T. Lambert, President, The Toronto-Dominion Bank
Radcliffe R. Latimer, President and Chief Executive Officer, TransCanada Pipelines Ltd.
Dr. D.S.R. Leighton, Professor, School of Business Administration, The University of Western Ontario
Pierre Lortie, Chairman and Chief Executive Officer, Provigo Inc.
George S. MacDonell, Deputy Minister, Ministry of Industry & Trade
Peter Maurice, President and Chief Executive Officer, Canada Trust
H. Harrison McCain, Chairman, McCain Foods Limited
Donald K. McIvor, Chairman and Chief Executive Officer, Imperial Oil Ltd.
Fred H. McNeil, President, Bank of Montreal
Donald H. McPherson, President and General Manager, General Motors of Canada Limited
Professor Al Mikalachki, Associate Dean (Programs), School of Business Administration, The University of Western Ontario
Arthur H. Mingay, Chairman and Chief Executive Officer, The Canada Trust Company
Jean C. Monty, President and Chief Executive Officer, Bell Canada
John H. Moore, President, John Labatt Ltd.
Trevor F. Moore, Vice-President, Imperial Oil Ltd.
J. Dean Muncaster, President, Canadian Tire Corporation Limited
Michael J. Needham, President, Helix Investments Limited
J. Edward M. Newall, Chairman, President and Chief Executive Officer, Du Pont Canada Inc.
Robert E.M. Nourse, President and Chief Executive Officer, The Bombay Company, Inc.
Earl H. Orser, President and Chief Executive Officer, London Life Insurance Company
G.F. Osbaldeston, Secretary, Ministry of State for Economic Development
Professor David A. Peach, Associate Dean (Human Resources), School of Business Administration, The University of Western Ontario
George A. Peapples, President and General Manager, General Motors of Canada Limited
Dr. K. George Pedersen, President and Vice-Chancellor, The University of Western Ontario
J.A. Pollock, President, Electrohome Limited
Alfred Powis, Esq., President, Noranda Mines Limited
W.H. Rea, (Chairman) Chairman of the Board, Great Canadian Oil Sands Limited
Robert H. Reid, President and Managing Director, The London Life Insurance Company
Bruce H. Reid, President and Chief Executive Officer, The Brick Warehouse Corporation

S.S. Reisman, Deputy Minister, Finance, Department of Finance
Grant L. Reuber, Deputy Chairman and Deputy Chief Executive Officer, Bank of Montreal
Cedric E. Ritchie, Chairman, President and Chief Executive Officer, The Bank of Nova Scotia
The Honourable John P. Robarts, Q.C., Stikeman, Elliott, Robarts and Bowman
R.G. Rogers, President, Crown Zellerbach Corporation Limited
E.R. Rowzee, President and Managing Director, Polymer Corporation Ltd.
Ian C. Rush, President and Chief Executive Officer, Polysar Limited
Donald C. Scott, Clarkson, Gordon & Co.
Karl E. Scott, President, The Ford Motor Company of Canada Limited
R.C. Scrivener, Chairman of the Board and Chief Executive Officer, Bell Canada
C. Richard Sharpe, Chairman and Chief Executive Officer, Simpsons-Sears Limited
Professor David C. Shaw, Associate Dean, School of Business Administration, The University of Western Ontario
A.E. Shepherd, Esq., Barrister
Frank T. Sherk, Esq., Industrialist
Helen K. Sinclair, President, The Canadian Bankers' Association
F. Alan Smith, President and General Manager, General Motors of Canada Limited
Leroy D. Smithers, President, Dow Chemical of Canada Ltd.
Dr. Michael D. Sopko, Chairman and Chief Executive Officer, Inco Limited
Dr. W.J. Stenason, Vice-President Transport and Ships, Canadian Pacific
James A. Stewart, Esq., Continental Can International Corp.
William G. Stewart, President and Chief Executive Officer, Union Gas Ltd.
J. Allyn Taylor, President and General Manager, Canada Trust-Huron & Erie
R.B. Taylor, Vice-President and Treasurer, The Steel Co. of Canada Ltd.
Paul Tellier, Clerk of the Privy Council & Secretary to the Cabinet
Walter A. Thompson, Associate Dean, School of Business Administration, The University of Western Ontario
John M. Thompson, President and Chief Executive Officer, IBM Canada Ltd.
The Hon. K.R. Thomson, Times Newspapers Limited
Nancy Thomson, President, Investing for Women
George M. Tidball, President, Keg Restaurants Ltd.
Marcel Vincent, Esq., Chairman, Bell Canada
J. Leonard Walker, Esq., President, Bank of Montreal
F.W. Walker Jr., General Manager, Diesel Division, General Motors of Canada Limited
Lt. Col. D.B. Weldon, Chairman, Midland-Osler Corporation Ltd., Chairman, Board of Governors
David B. Weldon, President, Midland-Osler Securities Ltd.
John J. Wettlaufer, Dean, School of Business Administration, The University of Western Ontario
J.R. White, Director, Standard Oil New Jersey, Honorary Member, Advisory Committee
Peter N.T. Widdrington, President and Chief Executive Officer, John Labatt Limited
William P. Wilder, President, Wood Gundy Securities Ltd.
D. Carlton Williams, President and Vice-Chancellor, The University of Western Ontario
Ross B. Willis, Vice-President, The University of Western Ontario, Member, Board of Governors
B.F. Willson, President and Chief Executive Officer, Union Gas Company of Canada Limited
R.D. Wolfe, Chairman of the Board and Chief Executive Officer, The Oshawa Group Limited
J.E. Woods, President, The Monarch Life Assurance Company
Larry Wynant, Associate Dean, Western Business School, The University of Western Ontario
W.M. Young, Chairman and Chief Executive Officer, Finning Tractor and Equipment Company Limited

# Current Members of Advisory Committee

John S. Brant, Goliger's Travel

Thomas H. Brent, Chairman and Chief Executive Officer, Brent Surgical Inc.

Robert D. Brown, Chairman and Senior Partner, Price Waterhouse

Claude Bruneau, President, San Palo Investments Corporation

C. David Clark, Chairman and Publisher, Globe and Mail

Brendan R. Clouston, Executive Vice-President and Chief Operating Officer, Tele-Communications, Inc.

George B. Cobbe, Managing Director of North American Operations, Hewlett-Packard Company

Richard J. Currie, President, Loblaw Companies Ltd.

Paul G. Desmarais, Chairman and Chief Executive Officer, Power Corporation of Canada

Brian P. Drummond, Vice-Chairman, Richardson Greenshields of Canada Ltd.

Robert A. Ferchat, Chairman and Chief Executive Officer, TMI Communications

Geno F. Francolini, President, Xenon Capital Corporation

Barbara H. Fraser, Vice-President and General Manager Beauty Care Products, Procter & Gamble Inc.

R. Donald Fullerton, Chairman - Executive Committee, Canadian Imperial Bank of Commerce

Jon K. Grant, Chairman of the Board, The Quaker Oats Company of Canada Ltd.

Professor Kenneth G. Hardy, Associate Dean and Director, NCMRD, Western Business School, The University of Western Ontario

Kenneth W. Harrigan

Wilbert H. Hopper

Richard W. Ivey, Chairman, Livingston Group Inc.

Professor Charles B. Johnston, Western Business School, The University of Western Ontario

Professor Peter Killing, Associate Dean, Western Business School, The University of Western Ontario

Gerald L. Knowlton, Chairman, Knowlton Realty Limited

Peter Maurice, President and Chief Executive Officer, Canada Trust

H. Harrison McCain, Chairman, McCain Foods Limited

Jean C. Monty, President and Chief Executive Officer, Northern Telecom Ltd.

J. Dean Muncaster, President, Environmental Technologies International Inc.

Michael J. Needham, President, Interactive Simulation Inc.

Robert E.M. Nourse, President and Chief Executive Officer, The Bombay Company, Inc.

Earl H. Orser, Chairman of the Board, London Life Insurance Company

Dr. K. George Pedersen, President and Vice-Chancellor, The University of Western Ontario

Bruce H. Reid, President and Chief Executive Officer, The Brick Warehouse Corporation

Grant L. Reuber, Chairman, Canada Deposit Insurance Corporation

Cedric E. Ritchie, Chairman and Chief Executive Officer, The Bank of Nova Scotia

Professor Adrian B. Ryans, Dean, Western Business School, The University of Western Ontario

Donald C. Scott

C. Richard Sharpe, Chairman, Sears Canada Inc.

Helen K. Sinclair, President, The Canadian Bankers' Association

Dr. Michael D. Sopko, Chairman and Chief Executive Officer, Inco Ltd.

Allan R. Taylor, Chairman and Chief Executive Officer, The Royal Bank of Canada

Paul Tellier, President and Chief Executive Officer, Canadian National Railway Company

Nancy G. Thomson, Chair, Nancy Thomson Investing For Women

George M. Tidball, G.M. Tidball & Associates

Peter N.T. Widdrington, Chairman, Toronto Blue Jays Baseball Club and Chairman, Laidlaw Inc.

Professor Larry Wynant, Associate Dean, Western Business School, The University of Western Ontario

# Honorary Members of Advisory Committee

John A. Armstrong

Ralph M. Barford

John E. Brent

G. Allan Burton

Richard M. Ivey, Q.C.

Captain Joseph Jeffery, Q.C.

William P. Wilder

# THE WESTERN BUSINESS SCHOOL COMMUNITY

## Leaders of the School

| | |
|---|---|
| **1922 - 1929** | **Ellis Morrow**, Head, Department of Commercial Economics |
| **1929 - 1938** | **Philip H. Hensel**, Head, Department of Business Administration |
| **1938 - 1942** | **Walter A. Thompson**, Acting Head, Department of Business Administration |
| **1942 - 1946** | **Ross B. Willis**, Acting Head, Department of Business Administration |
| **1946 - 1950** | **Walter A. Thompson**, Acting Head, Department of Business Administration |
| **1950 - 1954** | **Lloyd W. Sipherd**, Dean, School of Business Administration |
| **1954 - 1963** | **Frederick W.P. Jones**, Dean, School of Business Administration |
| **1963 - 1978** | **John J. Wettlaufer**, Dean, School of Business Administration |
| **1978 - 1989** | **Charles B. Johnston**, Dean, School of Business Administration |
| **1989 - 1990** | **Alexander Mikalachki**, Acting Dean, School of Business Administration |
| **1990 - present** | **Adrian B. Ryans**, Dean, Western Business School |

## Current and Past Members of the Western Business School Community

Thomas Abel
Neil Abramson
David Ager
Larry Agranove
Chris Albinson
Douglas Allen
Donald Amoroso
Jay Anand
Mark Applebaum
Lisa Applebaum
Ross Archibald
Neil Armstrong
Stephen Ash
Leslie Atkin
Gordon Avard
Patricia Avery
Connie Badame
Mark Baetz
Donald Barclay
R. Barrett
Greg Barron
James Bartos
Peggy Bateman

Nancy Batty
Clair Batty
Richard Bauer Jr.
Doreen Bayley
Paul Beamish
Carol Beaune
Patricia Beccarea
Moira Beedling
Charles Bell
Peter Bell
Nigel Bellchamber
Beryl Ben-Reuven
Karan Bennett
Karen Bennett
Winnifred Beno
Jill Benson
William Benson
Dale Bent
Paul Bergman
Mary Jane Bertin
Jeff Bertrand
J. Betterley
Kari Beukema

Peter Biesiot
Elizabeth Bishop
Paul Bishop
Clara Black
Carol Blackwell
Allan Blair
Nels Blair
Richard Blake
Kenneth Bobele
John Boersema
Patti Bogart
Robert Bolf
Omar Bolli
Mary Boniface
Brant Bonner
Pauline Boothroyd
Frances Bourne
Gary Boydell
Robert Bracey
Mark Bramwell
Helen Braxton
Beatrice Brewer
Christopher Bridgnell

Cheryl Briglia
Julia Bristor
Robert Britney
Caroline Brohman
Bonnie Brooke
George Brooks
Elizabeth Brown
Jan Brown
Sue Brown
William Brown
Barry Bruce
Edward Bugeja
Nola Buhr
Shirley Bullas
Nona Bulmer
David Burgoyne
Cathy Burgoyne
David Burrell
James Butler
Elaine Calder
Al Caldwell
Violet Caldwell
Edith Caldwell

Catherine Campbell
Cliff Campbell
Marilyn Campbell
Neil Campbell
Sigrid Campbell
Ann Carden
Cecil Carrothers
Oekie Carrothers
Michael Carter
Tupper Cawsey
Murray Cayley
Ross Chafe
Angela Challenor
Barbara Chatten
Peter Chiaramonte
D'Orcy Clare
Doug Clark
Yvonne Clarke
Deborah Clary
Denis Coleman
Deborah Compeau
Wendy Comstock
David Conklin
Michael Conlin
Janis Connolly
Janet Connor
R. Consler
Randall Cook
Stan Cook
Bonnie Cooper
Duncan Copeland
Catherine Copp
Virginia Corner
Steven Cox
Harold Crookell
Mary Crossan
Gordon Cudmore
Norene Culp
John Cummings
Barbara Cunningham
Frank Curran
John Currie
Sue Danowski
Connie Darling
Lisa Davidson

Dorothy Davies
Lester Davis
Gary Davis
George Day
Louise Day
Robert Deane
Mary Anne de
    Kergommeaux
Michelle Delellis
Terry Deutscher
Jim deWilde
Penny Dickenson
Sheila Dillon
Tony Dimnik
Joe DiStefano
Linda Dittmer-Pino
Renata Djurfeldt
Olive Dodds
C. Donohue
Jeff Dossett
Robin Dow
Carol Down
P. Downing
David Drinkwalter
John Dromgole
Clarende Duby
Robyn Duke
Theresa Dunbar
Kenneth Dundas
Watson Dunn
Andrew Durnford
Errol Duval
Lori Eardley
George Edwards
Ada Edwards
Marlene Eeley
James Ellert
Nancy Ellery
Judy Ellis
Virginia Elston
Bob Engel
Rhonda English
James Erskine
Elizabeth Facey
Robert Falconer

Peter Farrell
Barbara Farrugia
Nikolai Fartuch
Richard Faryon
Sally Fawcett
Richard Ferguson
Desmond ffolliott
Paul Fife
Doug Finley
Dolores Finnigan
Joan Firth
Jean Fish
Marlene Fitzgerald
James Fleck
Monica Fleck
Andrew Fletcher
Stephen Foerster
Graeme Fogelberg
George Forsyth
Edward Fox
Ann Francescon
Geno Francolini
Harold Frankiel
Clarence Fraser
Colette Frayne
Betty Freeborn
Kim Frenette
Lawrence Fric
Nick Fry
Carol Fuller
Michael Fuller
Candy Gadwa
Donna Gallina
Larysa Gamula
Jeffrey Gandz
Betty Ann Garside
Fredrick Genzmer
Michael Geringer
Christine Gibson
Janis Gilbert
Mary-Louise Giles
Clark Gilmour
Donna Gingras
Kathy Girden
James Girvin

Sheila Givens
Jean Goldie
Betty Golding
Peter Goldthorpe
John Gordon
Christopher Graham
John Graham
Nancy Graham
Mary Jane Grant
Erma Gras
Elizabeth Grasby
Monty Gray
Terry Green
Sheryl Gregson
Scott Griffith
Andrew Grindlay
Michael Guolla
Christoph Haehling von
    Lanzenauer
Michael Hagerman
Nicole Haggerty
John Hamilton
Nina Hanck
Thomas Handley
James Hanson
Kenneth Hardy
Brenda Harrison
Martha Harrower
Jean Harvey
Cheryl Harvey
James Hatch
A. Hawes
Rosina Hawthorne
Nadine Hayes
John Haywood-Farmer
Sonya Head
Julie Heal
Karen Heatherley
Joseph Heffernan
Mark Heisz
Fay Henderson
Janette Henry
Yvonne Henry
Phillip Hensel
David Herskowitz

Cam Hicks
Barry Hicks
Christopher Higgins
Gerald Higgins
Kevin Higgins
Terry Hildebrand
J. Hill
Kerry Hill
Neil Hill
Richard Hobbs
Thomas Hockin
Margaret Hodgins
Ross Hodgins
Richard Hodgson
Jamie Horn
Carol Howard
John Howard
Jane Howell
Sidney Huff
Linda Hughes
Helen Huitema
John Hulland
John Humphrey
Karen Humphreys
Hugh Hunter
Alexandra Hurst
David Hurst
Roy Hurst
Gordon Huson
Mary Hussey
David Husson
Dana Hyde
Andrew Inkpen
Helen Innes
John Irwin
Danielle Isber
J. Jackson
Phyllis Jackson
Stephen Jakob
Nancy Jamieson
E. Jarmain
Edwin Jarmain
Paul Jarvis
John Jeffs
Peter Jeffs

Michael Jensen
Cathy Jillard
H. Thomas Johnson
Irene Johnson
Charles B. Johnston
Una Johnston
Laurie Johnston
Brian Jones
Frederick Jones
Peter Jones
Barbara Jordan
Joseph Kairys
John Kamauff
Lambros Karavis
Janet Karn
Susan Karn
Karen Katsiroumbas
Cheryl Kay
Hope Keddy
Michael Kennedy
John Kennedy
Ernest Kepper
George Kerr
Jean Ann Kerr
Judith Kerr
Peter Killing
Carole Kinahan
Janet King
Thomas Kinnear
Peter Kirkham
Layne Kirkpatrick
Paul Kirkpatrick
Deborah Kleiman
Leo Klus
Ida Kmiec
Lynn Knight
Judy Knight
Russell Knight
Pamela Knoblauch
Peter Knobloch
Maria Knowles
Dennis Konchak
Lorrie Kope
Karen Korpan-Frosst
Suzann Kovacs

Susanna Kraus
Jasna Krympotic
Beata Krzynowek
Randolph Kudar
David Kuechle
Rudi Kuhlman
Kirklyn Kuzdrall
Paul Kuzdrall
Hero L'ecuyer
Dwight Ladd
Stanley Laiken
Ronald Lalonde
Douglas Lambert
Rick Lancaster
Henry Lane
Claude Lanfranconi
Susan Lansdell
Stephannie Larocque
Wallace Laut
Justin Lavallee
Jean Law
Rosemary Lawrence-Pitt
Burton Leathers
Stephen Lebner
Donald Lecraw
Raymond Leduc
Diana Lee
Sarah Lee
Michiel Leenders
Ronald Lefebvre
Alanna Leffley
Holly Legros
David Leighton
Charles Lemmon
Sue LeMoine
Beverley Lennox
Janet Leslie
Michael Levenhagen
JoAnn Lewis
Richard Lewis
Veronica Libby
Carl Lindros
Rita Lingner
Michelle Linton
Jack Lintott

Blair Little
Judy Little
Cheryl Lojzer
Robert Long
Stephen Long
Michael Longlade
Robert Lord
Kenneth Loucks
Elia Loutfy
Mary Ann Lowry
Lisa Luinenburg
Craig Lundberg
Eric Lutz
Connie Mabb
Sharon MacArthur
Ann MacDonald
Fraser MacDonald
John Macdonald
Joan MacDonald
Norman MacIntosh
James Mackay
Helen MacMillan
Christine MacNeil
Sharon Mahon
Claudia Mahoney
Renata Mak
Robert Malanchuk
Leena Malik
Marianne Malo
Jessie Marks
Lynn Marples
Floyd Marshall
Lawrence Martello
Anne Martin
Heather Martin
Samuel Martin
Lynn Maslen
James Mason
Elizabeth Masson
Frank Mastrandrea
Louise Maufette-Leenders
Kennedy May
Sandra McArdle
John McArthur
Sharon McArthur

| | | | |
|---|---|---|---|
| Pat McCabe | Leanne Nelson | Tracey Paul | Carol Riley |
| Lynn McClary | Richard Nesbitt | Ingrid Pawley | Jean Ann Rioux |
| A. McDermid | Sharon Neupert | David Peach | John Robarts |
| Douglas McDonald | J. Newbould | Gordon Pearce | Janice Roberts |
| Jack McDougall | Harold Newell | Michael Pearce | Mary Roberts |
| P. A. McDougall | Julie Newby | Bruce Pearson | Todd Roberts |
| Anne McFarland | David Newhouse | Peggy Pepper | Darroch Robertson |
| Patricia McKay | Peter Newson | Loretta Peregrina | Jean Robertson |
| Gordon McKee | John Nicholson | Melinda Perry | Nonie Robinson |
| Walter McKibben | Patricia Nicholson | Penny Peter | Ruth Rosen |
| Cynthia McLean | Marianne Nightingale | D. Paul Peters | Rosemary Rosier |
| Dennis McLeavey | James Nininger | Mary E. Peterson | Mitchell Rothstein |
| Karry McLellan | Detlev Nitsch | Mary J. Peterson | Brenda Rouse |
| Jay McLeod | Aldine Nixon | Rein Peterson | Fraser Rowland |
| Carol McNabb | Beverly Nixon | Barbara Pinder | Elain Runalls |
| James McNee | Peter Nixon | Christopher Piper | James Rush |
| Patricia Medeiros | Jackie Nguyen | John Pliniussen | Heather Russell |
| Lisa Melnychyn | Richard Nobbs | Barbara Pokropek | Adrian Ryans |
| Al Mikalachki | Margot Northey | Priscilla Pooler | Doreen Sanders |
| Judy Miller | Fred Norwood | Bernard Portis | Margaret Saunders |
| Richard Mimick | Laura Nother | Robert Potters | Sonya Scarrow |
| Linda Minutillo | Robert Nourse | Kathryn Pottruff | Corry Scott |
| Louise Mirlin | Sue O'Driscoll | Anne Powell | Gregory Scott |
| Brad Moon | Diane Olekson | Thomas Poynter | Karen Scott |
| Milan Moravec | Dale Oliver | Gail Prenger | Mark Scott |
| Roger More | Nelda Oman | John Preston | Karen Scrivens |
| Sidney Morehouse | Donald Ong | Kenneth Price | John Sears |
| Carol Moreno | Mitch Orr | B. Pumple | Marilyn Senft |
| Ivor Morgan | Tom Orr | Bill Pursell | David Sharp |
| Ieuan Morgan | Robert Orser | Terry Pursell | David Shaw |
| Joanne Morgan | Gordon Osbaldeston | John Quelch | Gary Sheehan |
| Allen Morrison | David Osborn | Cathy Quick | Lynne Sheridan |
| Donna Morrison | Gilles Ouellette | Barbara Quinn | Glenwood Shetter |
| Ellis Morrow | Barbara Owan | Russell Radford | Jill Shields |
| Stephen Moss | Francis Oxley | Lennie Rae | Anna Showler |
| Susan Munoz | JoAnne Palmateer | Alan Raedels | John Siambani |
| George Munro | David Palmer | Susan Ram | Leslie Sigouin |
| Hugh Munro | Earl Palmer | Marjorie Rand | Penny Sim |
| Helen Murray | Kathleen Panabaker | Anne Rasmussen | Donald Simpson |
| Jeffrey Murray | Peggy Pardo | Robert Ready | Beth Sinclair |
| John Myers | Margaret Park | Margaret Reffle | Jeanette Sinclair |
| Helen Myles | Deborah Parkes | Betty Rennie | Pamela Sinfield |
| Pat Neatby | Joan Patrick | Pauline Renpenning | Lloyd Sipherd |
| William Nediger | Reginald Patterson | Peter Richardson | Tracey Skinkle |
| Jody Neely | John Pattison | Pauline Riddell | Malcolm Slaght |

Kathleen Slaughter
Derrick Sloan
Angela Smith
Donald Smith
Paul Smith
Sherry Smugler
Patricia Sobeski
Ernie Spence
Robert Springett
Robert Sproule
Charles Spry
Winston St. Clair
Katherine St.John
Mary Stackhouse-Hatt
Roy Stainton
Erle Steiss
Judy Steven
Daphne Stevens
Joan Stevens
Kathleen Stevens
Ronald Stevens
Stuart Stevens
Leanna Stewart
Mary Stopar
Ron Storey
Sharon Story
Jean Strangways
Ella Strong

Jean Sutherland
Douglas Tait
Irene Tapley
James C. Taylor
Robert Taylor
Gerri Teal
Howard Teall
Donald Thain
Darlene Thomas
Walter Thompson
Evelyn Toman
Lorrie Tomas
Helen Tomlinson
David Town
Anne Marie Traher
Alain D. Tuchmaier
Frances Tyrrell
Wayne Ullerick
Herb Uren
Dorothy Van Bommel
Marianne Vandenbosch
Mark Vandenbosch
Robert VanderWees
Peter Vanexan
Emily VanHoutte
Cyndi van Rossum
Christine Veber
Linda Verde

Kate Vickery
W. Volk
Mary Jane Vonesh
Naomi Vonesh
Chris Voss
Deborah Vuylsteke
Florence Wachowiak
Donald Wallace
John Walsh
Timothy Warner
Joseph Washington
Jackie Watson
Barbara Waugh
Robert Waugh
Mark Webb
Wesley Weber
Arnold Weinstein
Rick Wellard
James Westervelt
Jeannette Weston
Gaye Weston
John Wettlaufer
Mark Wettlaufer
John White
Lynda White
Robert White
Roderick White
Joan Whiteford

David Whitehead
Edmund Whittaker
Mary Wilkes
Steve Wilkinson
Angela Williamson
David Williamson
Linda Willis
Ross Willis
Ronald Wirick
Mark Wisternoff
Sharon Withenshaw
Ronald J. Wonnacott
Thomas Wonnacott
Albert Wood
William Wood
Jerry Woods
Ken Woytaz
Ruth Wright
Leonard Wrigley
Larry Wynant
Nicholas Yarmoshuk
Kevin Yousie
Friedrich Zabransky
Diane Zandri
Dorothy Zavitz
Connie Zrini

# Editors of the 'BQ'

The *Business Quarterly* evolved from the *Commerce Journal,* founded in the depths of a depression, by the undergraduates of the Commerce Club at Western and was edited by Lyle McKay, a Commerce student who obtained a grant to permit printing. Published for the first time in December of 1932, the seven-page mimeographed issue developed, over the years, into *Business Quarterly* a paid circulation publication which, in 1993, is one of Canada's leading, authoritative magazines devoted to the practice of management.

In the premier issue, W. Sherwood Fox in his "Message from the President" wrote, with uncanny clairvoyance, the following:

"A carefully edited journal of this type can achieve many things. As a printed outlet of studies of real business problems it can keep businessmen informed as to what the University is doing in paving the undergraduate's approach to actual business. Occasionally it may be so fortunate as to suggest, or even outline, to a business concern the practical solution of a problem. It can become the recorder of permanent messages, to be read and pondered upon at leisure, from business itself to those who aspire to enter business. These illustrations suffice to show what great promise may be latent in the few pages of the first number of a timely publication. Who then can predict the future of the *Commerce Journal?* In time it may develop into a great and influential business review."

## EDITORS

**Published by University Students' Commission and the Commerce Club**

| | |
|---|---|
| 1932-'33 | Lyle McKay |
| 1933-'34 | A.G. Merrifield |
| 1934-'35 | Brock Short |
| 1935-'37 | Thomas H. Orr |
| 1937-'38 | James C. Taylor |
| 1938-'39 | Ross Anderson |
| 1939-'40 | Austin Conway |
| 1941-'41 | Jay Cameron |
| 1942 | Ray Keelan |
| | W.F. Steeper |
| | Elaine Doherty *Consulting Editor* |

**Published by Departments of Business Administration and Political Science**

| | |
|---|---|
| 1942 | R. Burns |
| 1943 | Byron Boughner |
| 1944 | John Cooper |
| 1945 | Daniel Thompson |
| 1945-'47 | R.B. Taylor |
| 1947-'50 | W.R. Waugh |

**Published by School of Business Administration**

| | |
|---|---|
| 1949 | D.H. Ong |
| 1950 | Martha Harrower *Managing Editor* |
| 1951-'54 | Dwight R. Ladd |
| 1954-'58 | Gordon Huson |
| 1959-'61 | David Leighton |
| 1961-'69 | Jack McDougall |
| 1963-'70 | Doreen Sanders *Managing Editor* |
| 1970-'88 | Doreen Sanders |
| 1988- | Andrew Grindlay |

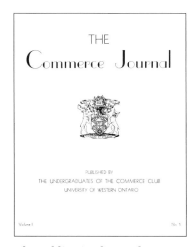  

The publication has undergone a number of format and title changes: *Quarterly Review of Commerce; Business Quarterly* to its present *BQ – Business Quarterly.*

VERITAS ET UTILITAS